Quantitative Trading

Founded in 1807, John Wiley & Sons is the oldest independent publishing company in the United States. With offices in North America, Europe, Australia, and Asia, Wiley is globally committed to developing and marketing print and electronic products and services for our customers' professional and personal knowledge and understanding.

The Wiley Trading series features books by traders who have survived the market's ever changing temperament and have prospered—some by reinventing systems, others by getting back to basics. Whether a novice trader, professional, or somewhere in-between, these books will provide the advice and strategies needed to prosper today and well into the future.

For a list of available titles, visit our Web site at www.WileyFinance.com.

Quantitative Trading

How to Build Your Own Algorithmic Trading Business

ERNEST P. CHAN

WILEY

John Wiley & Sons, Inc.

Published by John Wiley & Sons, Inc., Hoboken, New Jersey.
Published simultaneously in Canada.

For general information on our other products and services or for technical support, please contact our Customer Care Department within the United States at (800) 762-2974, outside the United States at (317) 572-3993 or fax (317) 572-4002.

Wiley also publishes its books in a variety of electronic formats. Some content that appears in print may not be available in electronic books. For more information about Wiley products, visit our web site at www.wiley.com.

Library of Congress Cataloging-in-Publication Data

Chan, Ernest P.
    Quantitative trading: how to build your own algorithmic trading business / Ernest P. Chan.
        p. cm.–(Wiley trading series)
    Includes bibliographical references and index.
    ISBN 978-0-470-28488-9 (cloth)
    1. Investment analysis.   2. Stocks.   3. Stockbrokers.   I. Title.
    HG4529.C445   2009
    332.64–dc22

                                                                    2008020125

Printed in the United States of America.

16

To my parents Hung Yip and Ching, and to Ben.

Contents

Preface

By some estimates, quantitative or algorithmic trading now accounts for over one-third of the trading volume in the United States. There are, of course, innumerable books on the advanced mathematics and strategies utilized by institutional traders in this arena. However, can an independent, retail trader benefit from these algorithms? Can an individual with limited resources and computing power backtest and execute their strategies over thousands of stocks, and come to challenge the powerful industry participants in their own game?

I will show you how this can, in fact, be achieved.

WHO IS THIS BOOK FOR?

I wrote this book with two types of readers in mind:

1. Aspiring independent ("retail") traders who are looking to start a quantitative trading business.
2. Students of finance or other technical disciplines (at the undergraduate or MBA level) who aspire to become quantitative traders and portfolio managers at major institutions.

Can these two very different groups of readers benefit from the same set of knowledge and skills? Is there anything common between managing a $100 million portfolio and managing a $100,000 portfolio? My contention is that it is much more logical and sensible for someone to become a profitable $100,000 trader before becoming a profitable $100 million trader. This can be shown to be true on many fronts.

Many legendary quantitative hedge fund managers such as Dr. Edward Thorp of the former Princeton-Newport Partners (Poundstone, 2005) and Dr. Jim Simons of Renaissance Technologies Corp. (Lux, 2000) started their careers trading their own money. They did not begin as portfolio managers for investment banks and hedge funds before starting their own fund management business. Of course, there are also plenty of counterexamples, but clearly this is a possible route to riches as well as intellectual accomplishment, and for someone with an entrepreneurial bent, a preferred route.

Even if your goal is to become an institutional trader, it is still worthwhile to start your own trading business as a first step. Physicists and mathematicians are now swarming Wall Street. Few people on the Street are impressed by a mere PhD from a prestigious university anymore. What is the surest way to get through the door of the top banks and funds? To show that you have a systematic way to profits—in other words, a track record. Quite apart from serving as a stepping stone to a lucrative career in big institutions, having a profitable track record as an independent trader is an invaluable experience in itself. The experience forces you to focus on simple but profitable strategies, and not get sidetracked by overly theoretical or sophisticated theories. It also forces you to focus on the nitty-gritty of quantitative trading that you won't learn from most books: things such as how to build an order entry system that doesn't cost $10,000 of programming resource. Most importantly, it forces you to focus on risk management—after all, your own personal bankruptcy is a possibility here. Finally, having been an institutional as well as a retail quantitative trader and strategist at different times, I only wish that I had read a similar book before I started my career at a bank—I would have achieved profitability many years sooner.

Given these preambles, I won't make any further apologies in the rest of the book in focusing on the entrepreneurial, independent traders and how they can build a quantitative trading business on their own, while hoping that many of the lessons would be useful on their way to institutional money management as well.

WHAT KIND OF BACKGROUND DO YOU NEED?

Despite the scary-sounding title, you don't need to be a math or computer whiz in order to use this book as a guide to start trading quantitatively. Yes, you do need to possess some basic knowledge of statistics, such as how to calculate averages, standard deviations, or how to fit a straight line through a set of data points. Yes, you also need to have some basic familiarity with Excel. But what you don't need is any advanced knowledge of stochastic calculus, neural networks, or other impressive-sounding techniques.

Though it is true that you can make millions with nothing more than Excel, it is also true that there is another tool that, if you are proficient at it, will enable you to backtest trading strategies much more efficiently, and may also allow you to retrieve and process data much more easily than you otherwise can. This tool is called MATLAB®, and it is a mathematical platform that many institutional quantitative strategists and portfolio managers use. Therefore, I will demonstrate how to backtest the majority of strategies using MAT-LAB. In fact, I have included a brief tutorial in the appendix on how to do some basic programming in MATLAB. For many retail traders, MATLAB is too expensive to purchase, but there are cheaper alternatives, which I will mention in Chapter 3 on backtesting. Furthermore, many university students can either purchase a cheaper student MATLAB license or they already have free access to it through their schools.

WHAT WILL YOU FIND IN THIS BOOK?

This book is definitely not designed as an encyclopedia of quantitative trading techniques or terminologies. It will not even be about specific profitable strategies (although you can refine the few example strategies embedded here to make them quite profitable.) Instead, this is a book that teaches you how to find a profitable strategy yourself. It teaches you the characteristics of a good strategy, how to refine and backtest a strategy to ensure that it has good historical performance, and, more importantly, to ensure that it will remain profitable in the future. It teaches you a systematic way to scale up or wind down your strategies depending on their real-life profitability. It teaches you some of the nuts and bolts of implementing an automated execution system in your own home. Finally, it teaches you some basics of risk management, which is critical if you want to survive over the long term, and also some psychological pitfalls to avoid if you want an enjoyable (and not just profitable) life as a trader.

Even though the basic techniques for finding a good strategy should work for any tradable securities, I have focused my examples on an area of trading I personally know best: statistical arbitrage trading in stocks. While I discuss sources of historical data on stocks, futures, and foreign currencies in the chapter on backtesting, I did not include options because those are not in my area of expertise.

The book is organized roughly in the order of the steps that traders need to undertake to set up their quantitative trading business. These steps begin at finding a viable trading strategy (Chapter 2), then backtesting the strategy to ensure that it at least has good historical performance (Chapter 3), setting up the business and technological infrastructure (Chapter 4), building an automated trading system to execute your strategy (Chapter 5), and managing the money and risks involved in holding positions generated by this strategy (Chapter 6). I will then describe in Chapter 7 a number of important advanced concepts with which most professional quantitative traders are familiar, and finally conclude in Chapter 8 with reflections on how independent traders can find their niche and how they can grow their business. I have also included an appendix that contains a tutorial on using MATLAB.

You'll see two different types of boxed material in this book:

- Sidebars containing an elaboration or illustration of a concept, and

- Examples, accompanied by MATLAB or Excel code.

For readers who want to learn more and keep up to date with the latest news, ideas, and trends in quantitative trading, they are welcome to visit my blog epchan.blogspot.com, where I will do my best to answer their questions, as well as my premium content web site epchan.com/subscriptions. My premium content web site contains articles of a more advanced nature, as well as backtest results of several profitable strategies. Readers of this book will have free access to the premium content and will find the password in a later chapter to enter that web site.

—Ernest P. Chan
Toronto, Ontario
August 2008

Acknowledgments

Much of my knowledge and experiences in quantitative trading come from my colleagues and mentors at the various investment banks (Morgan Stanley, Credit Suisse, Maple Securities) and hedge funds (Mapleridge Capital, Millennium Partners, MANE Fund Management), and I am very grateful for their advice, guidance, and help over the years. Since I became an independent trader and consultant, I have benefited enormously from discussions with my clients, readers of my blog, fellow bloggers, and various trader-collaborators. In particular, I would like to offer thanks to Steve Halpern and Ramon Cummins for reading parts of the manuscript and correcting some of the errors; to John Rigg for suggesting some of the topics for my blog, many of which found their way into this book; to Ashton Dorkins, editor-in-chief of tradingmarkets.com, who helped syndicate my blog; and to Yaser Anwar for publicizing it to readers of his own very popular investment blog. I am also indebted to editor Bill Falloon at John Wiley & Sons for suggesting this book, and to my development editor, Emilie Herman, and production editor Christina Verigan for seeing this book through to fruition. Last but not least, I thank Ben Xie for insisting that simplicity is the best policy.

E.P.C.

Quantitative Trading

CHAPTER 1

The Whats, Whos, and Whys of Quantitative Trading

I f you are curious enough to pick up this book, you probably have already heard of quantitative trading. But even for readers who learned about this kind of trading from the mainstream media before, it is worth clearing up some common misconceptions.

Quantitative trading, also known as algorithmic trading, is the trading of securities based strictly on the buy/sell decisions of computer algorithms. The computer algorithms are designed and perhaps programmed by the traders themselves, based on the historical performance of the encoded strategy tested against historical financial data.

Is quantitative trading just a fancy name for technical analysis, then? Granted, a strategy based on technical analysis can be part of a quantitative trading system if it can be fully encoded as computer programs. However, not all technical analysis can be regarded as quantitative trading. For example, certain chartist techniques such as "look for the formation of a head and shoulders pattern" might not be included in a quantitative trader's arsenal because they are quite subjective and may not be quantifiable.

Yet quantitative trading includes more than just technical analysis. Many quantitative trading systems incorporate fundamental data in their inputs: numbers such as revenue, cash flow, debt-to-equity ratio, and others. After all, fundamental data are nothing but numbers, and computers can certainly crunch any numbers that are fed into them! When it comes to judging the current financial performance of a company compared to its peers or compared to its historical performance, the computer is often just as good as human financial analysts—and the computer can watch thousands of such companies all at once. Some advanced quantitative systems can even incorporate news events as inputs: Nowadays, it is possible to use a computer to parse and understand the news report. (After all, I used to be a researcher in this very field at IBM, working on computer systems that can understand approximately what a document is about.)

So you get the picture: As long as you can convert information into bits and bytes that the computer can understand, it can be regarded as part of quantitative trading.

WHO CAN BECOME A QUANTITATIVE TRADER?

It is true that most institutional quantitative traders received their advanced degrees as physicists, mathematicians, engineers, or computer scientists. This kind of training in the hard sciences is often necessary when you want to analyze or trade complex derivative instruments. But those instruments are not the focus in this book. There is no law stating that one can become wealthy only by working with complicated financial instruments. (In fact, one can become quite poor trading complex mortgage-backed securities, as the financial crisis of 2007–08 and the demise of Bear Stearns have shown.) The kind of quantitative trading I focus on is called *statistical arbitrage trading*. Statistical arbitrage deals with the simplest financial instruments: stocks, futures, and sometimes currencies. One does *not* need an advanced degree to become a statistical arbitrage trader. If you have taken a few high school–level courses in math, statistics, computer programming, or economics, you are probably as qualified as anyone to tackle some of the basic statistical arbitrage strategies.

Okay, you say, you don't need an advanced degree, but surely it gives you an edge in statistical arbitrage trading? Not necessarily. I received a PhD from one of the top physics departments of the world (Cornell's). I worked as a successful researcher in one of the top computer science research groups in the world (at that temple of high-techdom: IBM's T. J. Watson Research Center). Then I worked in a string of top investment banks and hedge funds as a researcher and finally trader, including Morgan Stanley, Credit Suisse, and so on. As a researcher and trader in these august institutions, I had always strived to use some of the advanced mathematical techniques and training that I possessed and applied them to statistical arbitrage trading. Hundreds of millions of dollars of trades later, what was the result? Losses, more losses, and losses as far as the eye can see, for my employers and their investors. Finally, I quit the financial industry in frustration, set up a spare bedroom in my home as my trading office, and started to trade the simplest but still quantitative strategies I know. These are strategies that any smart high school student can easily research and execute. For the first time in my life, my trading strategies became profitable (one of which is described in Example 3.6), and has been the case ever since. The lesson I learned? As Einstein said: "Make everything as simple as possible." But not simpler.

(Stay tuned: I will detail more reasons why independent traders can beat institutional money managers at their own game in Chapter 8.)

Though I became a quantitative trader through a fairly traditional path, many others didn't. Who are the typical independent quantitative traders? Among people I know, they include a former trader at a hedge fund that has gone out of business, a computer programmer who used to work for a brokerage, a former trader at one of the exchanges, a former investment banker, a former biochemist, and an architect. Some of them have received advanced technical training, but others have only basic familiarity of high school–level statistics. Most of them backtest their strategies using basic tools like Excel, though others may hire programming contractors to help. Most of them have at some point in their career been professionally involved with the financial world but have now decided that being independent suits their needs better. As far as I know, most of them are doing quite well on their own, while enjoying the enormous freedom that independence brings.

Besides having gained some knowledge of finance through their former jobs, the fact that these traders have saved up a nest egg for their independent venture is obviously important too. When one plunges into independent trading, fear of losses and of being isolated from the rest of the world is natural, and so it helps to have both a prior appreciation of risks and some savings to lean on. It is important not to have a need for immediate profits to sustain your daily living, as strategies have intrinsic rates of returns that cannot be hurried (see Chapter 6).

Instead of fear, some of you are planning to trade because of the love of thrill and danger, or an incredible self-confidence that instant wealth is imminent. This is also a dangerous emotion to bring to independent quantitative trading. As I hope to persuade you in this chapter and in the rest of the book, instant wealth is not the objective of quantitative trading.

The ideal independent quantitative trader is therefore someone who has some prior experience with finance or computer programming, who has enough savings to withstand the inevitable losses and periods without income, and whose emotion has found the right balance between fear and greed.

THE BUSINESS CASE FOR QUANTITATIVE TRADING

A lot of us are in the business of quantitative trading because it is exciting, intellectually stimulating, financially rewarding, or perhaps it is the only thing we are good at doing. But for others who may have alternative skills and opportunities, it is worth pondering whether quantitative trading is the best business for you.

Despite all the talk about untold hedge fund riches and dollars that are measured in units of billions, in many ways starting a quantitative trading business is very similar to starting any small business. We need to start small, with limited investment (perhaps only a $50,000 initial investment), and gradually scale up the business as we gain know-how and become profitable.

In other ways, however, a quantitative trading business is very different from other small businesses. Here are some of the most important.

Scalability

Compared to most small businesses (other than certain dot-coms), quantitative trading is very scalable (up to a point). It is easy to find yourselves trading millions of dollars in the comfort of your own home, as long as your strategy is consistently profitable. This is because scaling up often just means changing a number in your program. This number is called *leverage.* You do not need to negotiate with a banker or a venture capitalist to borrow more capital for your business. The brokerages stand ready and willing to do that. If you are a member of a proprietary trading firm (more on this later in Chapter 4 on setting up a business), you may even be able to obtain a leverage far exceeding that allowed by Securities and Exchange Commission (SEC) Regulation T. It is not unheard of for a proprietary trading firm to let you trade a portfolio worth $2 million intraday even if you have only $50,000 equity in your account (a $\times 40$ leverage). At the same time, quantitative trading is definitely not a get-rich-quick scheme. You should hope to have steadily increasing profits, but most likely it won't be 200 percent a year, unlike starting a dot-com or a software firm. In fact, as I will explain in Chapter 6 on money and risk management, it is dangerous to overleverage in pursuit of overnight riches.

Demand on Time

Running most small businesses takes a lot of your time, at least initially. Quantitative trading takes relatively little of your time. By its very nature, quantitative trading is a highly automated business. Sometimes, the more you manually interfere with the system and override its decision, the worse it will perform. (Again, more on this in Chapter 6.)

How much time you need to spend on day-to-day quantitative trading depends very much on the degree of automation you have achieved. For example, at a hedge fund I used to work for, some colleagues come into the office only once a month. The rest of the time, they just sit at home and occasionally remotely monitor their office computers, which are trading for them.

I consider myself to be in the middle of the pack in terms of automation. The largest block of time I need to spend is in the morning before the market opens: I typically need to run various programs to download and process the latest historical data, read company news that comes up on my alert screen, run programs to generate the orders for the day, and then launch a few baskets of orders before the market opens and start a program that will launch orders automatically throughout the day. I would also update my spreadsheet to record the previous day's profit and loss (P&L) of the different strategies I run based on the brokerages' statements. All of this takes about two hours.

After that, I spend another half hour near the market close to direct the programs to exit various positions, manually checking that those exit orders are correctly transmitted, and closing down various automated programs properly.

In between market open and close, everything is supposed to be on autopilot. Alas, the spirit is willing but the flesh is weak: I often cannot resist the urge to take a look (sometimes many looks) at the intraday P&L of the various strategies on my trading screens. In extreme situations, I might even be transfixed by the huge swings in P&L and be tempted to intervene by manually exiting positions. Fortunately, I have learned to better resist the temptation as time goes on.

The urge to intervene manually is also strong when I have too much time on my hands. Hence, instead of just staring at your trading screen, it is actually important to engage yourself in some other, more healthful and enjoyable activities, such as going to the gym during the trading day.

When I said quantitative trading takes little of your time, I am referring to the operational side of the business. If you want to grow your business, or keep your current profits from declining due to increasing competition, you will need to spend time doing research and backtesting on new strategies. But research and development of new strategies is the creative part of any business, and it can be done whenever you want to. So, between the market's open and close, I do my research; answer e-mails; chat with other traders, collaborators, or clients; go to the gym; and so on. I do some of that work in the evening and on weekends, too, but only when I feel like it—not because I am obligated to.

When I generate more earnings, I will devote more software development resources to further automate my process, so that the programs can automatically start themselves up at the right time, know how to download data automatically, maybe even know how to interpret the news items that come across the newswire and take appropriate actions, and shut themselves down automatically after the market closes. When that day comes, the daily operation may take no time at all, and it can run as it normally does even while I am on vacation, as long as it can alert my mobile phone or a technical support service when something goes wrong. In short, if you treasure your leisure time or if you need time and financial resources to explore other businesses, quantitative trading is the business for you.

The Nonnecessity of Marketing

Here is the biggest and most obvious difference between quantitative trading and other small businesses. Marketing is crucial to most small businesses—after all, you generate your revenue from other people, who base their purchase decisions on things other than price alone. In trading, your counterparties in the financial marketplace base their purchase decisions on *nothing but* the price. Unless you are managing money for other people (which is beyond the scope of this book), there is absolutely no marketing to do in a quantitative trading business. This may seem obvious and trivial but is actually an important difference, since the business of quantitative trading allows you to focus exclusively on your product (the strategy and the software), and not on anything that has to do with influencing other people's perception of yourself. To many people, this may be the ultimate beauty of starting your own quantitative trading business.

THE WAY FORWARD

If you are convinced that you want to become a quantitative trader, a number of questions immediately follow: How do you find the right strategy to trade? How do you recognize a good versus a bad strategy even before devoting any time to backtesting them? How do you rigorously backtest them? If the backtest performance is good, what steps do you need to take to implement the strategy, in terms of both the business structure and the technological infrastructure? If the strategy is profitable in initial real-life trading, how does one scale up the capital to make it into a growing income stream while managing the inevitable (but, hopefully, only occasional) losses that come with trading? These nuts and bolts of quantitative trading will be tackled in Chapters 2 through 6.

Though the list of processes to go through in order to get to the final destination of sustained and growing profitability may seem long and daunting, in reality it may be faster and easier than many other businesses. When I first started as an independent trader, it took me only three months to find and backtest my first new strategy, set up a new brokerage account with $100,000 capital, implement the execution system, and start trading the strategy. The strategy immediately became profitable in the first month. Back in the dot-com era, I started an Internet software firm. It took about 3 times more investment, 5 times more human-power, and 24 times longer to find out that the business model didn't work, whereupon all investors including myself lost 100 percent of their investments. Compared to that experience, it really has been a breeze trading quantitatively and profitably.

CHAPTER 2

Fishing for Ideas

Where Can We Find Good Strategies?

This is the surprise: Finding a trading idea is actually *not* the hardest part of building a quantitative trading business. There are hundreds, if not thousands, of trading ideas that are in the public sphere at any time, accessible to anyone at little or no cost. Many authors of these trading ideas will tell you their complete methodologies in addition to their backtest results. There are finance and investment books, newspapers and magazines, mainstream media web sites, academic papers available online or in the nearest public library, trader forums, blogs, and on and on. Some of the ones I find valuable are listed in Table 2.1, but this is just a small fraction of what is available out there.

In the past, because of my own academic bent, I regularly perused the various preprints published by business school professors or downloaded the latest online finance journal articles to scan for good prospective strategies. In fact, the first strategy I traded when I became independent was based on such academic research. (It was a version of the PEAD strategy referenced in Chapter 7.) Increasingly, however, I have found that many strategies described by academics are either too complicated, out of date (perhaps the once-profitable strategies have already lost their power due to competition), or require expensive data to backtest (such as historical fundamental data). Furthermore, many of these academic

TABLE 2.1   Sources of Trading Ideas

Type	URL
Academic	
Business schools' finance professors' web sites	www.hbs.edu/research/research.html
Social Science Research Network	www.ssrn.com
National Bureau of Economic Research	www.nber.org
Business schools' quantitative finance seminars	www.ieor.columbia.edu/seminars/financialengineering
Mark Hulbert's column in the *New York Times*' Sunday business section	www.nytimes.com
Buttonwood column in the *Economist* magazine's finance section	www.economist.com
Financial web sites and blogs	
Yahoo! Finance	finance.yahoo.com
TradingMarkets	www.TradingMarkets.com
Seeking Alpha	www.SeekingAlpha.com
TheStreet.com	www.TheStreet.com
The Kirk Report	www.TheKirkReport.com
Alea Blog	www.aleablog.com
Abnormal Returns	www.AbnormalReturns.com
Brett Steenbarger Trading Psychology	www.brettsteenbarger.com
My own!	epchan.blogspot.com
Trader forums	
Elite Trader	www.Elitetrader.com
Wealth-Lab	www.wealth-lab.com
Newspaper and magazines	
Stocks, Futures and Options magazine	www.sfomag.com

strategies work only on small-cap stocks, whose illiquidity may render actual trading profits far less impressive than their backtests would suggest.

This is not to say that you will not find some gems if you are persistent enough, but I have found that many traders' forums or blogs may suggest simpler strategies that are equally profitable. You might be skeptical that people would actually post truly profitable strategies in the public space for all to see. After all, doesn't this disclosure increase the competition and decrease the profitability of the strategy? And you would be right: Most ready-made strategies that you may find in these places actually do not withstand careful backtesting. Just like the academic studies, the strategies from traders' forums may have worked only for a little while, or they work for only a certain class of stocks, or they work only if you don't factor in transaction costs. However, the trick is that you can often modify the basic strategy and make it profitable. (Many of these caveats as well as a few common variations on a basic strategy will be examined in detail in Chapter 3.)

For example, someone once suggested a strategy to me that was described in Wealth-Lab (see Table 2.1), where it was claimed that it had a high Sharpe ratio. When I backtested the strategy, it turned out not to work as well as advertised. I then tried a few simple modifications, such as decreasing the holding period and entering and exiting at different times than suggested, and was able to turn this strategy into one of my main profit centers. If you are diligent and creative enough to try the multiple variations of a basic strategy, chances are you will find one of those variations that is highly profitable.

When I left the institutional money management industry to trade on my own, I worried that I would be cut off from the flow of trading ideas from my colleagues and mentors. But then I found out that one of the best ways to gather and share trading ideas is to start your own trading blog—for every trading "secret" that you divulge to the world, you will be rewarded with multiple ones from your readers. (The person who suggested the Wealth-Lab strategy to me was a reader who works 12 time zones away. If it weren't for my blog, there was little chance that I would have met him and benefited from his suggestion.) In fact, what you thought of as secrets are more often than not well-known ideas to many others! What truly make a strategy proprietary and its secrets worth protecting are the tricks and variations that you have come up with, not the plain vanilla version.

Furthermore, your bad ideas will quickly get shot down by your online commentators, thus potentially saving you from major losses. After I glowingly described a seasonal stock-trading strategy on my blog that was developed by some finance professors, a reader promptly went ahead and backtested that strategy and reported that it didn't work. (See my blog entry, "Seasonal Trades in Stocks," at epchan.blogspot.com/2007/11/seasonal-trades-in-stocks.html and the reader's comment therein. This strategy is described in more detail in Example 7.6.) Of course, I would not have traded this strategy without backtesting it on my own anyway, and indeed, my subsequent backtest confirmed his findings. But the fact that my reader found significant flaws with the strategy is important confirmation that my own backtest is not erroneous.

All in all, I have found that it is actually easier to gather and exchange trading ideas as an independent trader than when I was working in the secretive hedge fund world in New York. (When I worked at Millennium Partners—a multibillion-dollar hedge fund on Fifth Avenue—one trader ripped a *published* paper out of the hands of his programmer, who happened to have picked it up from the trader's desk. He was afraid the programmer might learn his "secrets.") That may be because people are less wary of letting you know their secrets when they think you won't be obliterating their profits by allocating $100 million to that strategy.

No, the difficulty is not the lack of ideas. The difficulty is to develop a taste for which strategy is suitable for your personal circumstances and goals, and which ones look viable even before you devote the time to diligently backtest them. This taste for prospective strategies is what I will try to convey in this chapter.

HOW TO IDENTIFY A STRATEGY THAT SUITS YOU

Whether a strategy is viable often does not have anything to do with the strategy itself—it has to do with you. Here are some considerations.

Your Working Hours

Do you trade only part time? If so, you would probably want to consider only strategies that hold overnight and not the intraday strategies. Otherwise, you may have to fully automate your strategies (see Chapter 5 on execution) so that they can run on autopilot most of the time and alert you only when problems occur.

When I was working full time for others and trading part time for myself, I traded a simple strategy in my personal account that required entering or adjusting limit orders on a few exchange-traded funds (ETFs) once a day, before the market opened. Then, when I first became independent, my level of automation was still relatively low, so I considered only strategies that require entering orders once before the market opens and once before the close. Later on, I added a program that can automatically scan real-time market data and transmit orders to my brokerage account throughout the trading day when certain conditions are met. So trading remains a "part-time" pursuit for me, which is partly why I want to trade quantitatively in the first place.

Your Programming Skills

Are you good at programming? If you know some programming languages such as Visual Basic or even Java, C#, or C++, you can explore high-frequency strategies, and you can also trade a large number of securities. Otherwise, settle for strategies that trade only once a day, or trade just a few stocks, futures, or currencies. (This constraint may be overcome if you don't mind the expense of hiring a software contractor. Again, see Chapter 5 for more details.)

Your Trading Capital

Do you have a lot of capital for trading as well as expenditure on infrastructure and operation? In general, I would not recommend quantitative trading for an account with less than $50,000 capital. Let's say the dividing line between a high- versus low-capital account is $100,000. Capital availability affects many choices; the first is whether you should open a retail brokerage account or a proprietary trading account (more on this in Chapter 4 on setting up your business). For now, I will consider this constraint with strategy choices in mind.

With a low-capital account, we need to find strategies that can utilize the maximum leverage available. (Of course, getting a higher leverage is beneficial only if you have a consistently profitable strategy.) Trading futures, currencies, and options can offer you higher leverage than stocks; intraday positions allow a Regulation T leverage of 4, while interday (overnight) positions allow only a leverage of 2, requiring double the amount of capital for a portfolio of the same size. Finally, capital (or leverage) availability determines whether you should focus on directional trades (long or short only) or dollar-neutral trades (hedged or pair trades). A dollar-neutral portfolio (meaning the market value of the long positions equals the market value of the short positions) or market-neutral portfolio (meaning the *beta* of the portfolio with respect to a market index is close to zero, where *beta* measures the ratio between the expected returns of the portfolio and the expected returns of the market index) require twice the capital or leverage of a long- or short-only portfolio. So even though a hedged position is less risky than an unhedged position, the returns generated are correspondingly smaller and may not meet your personal requirements.

Capital availability also imposes a number of indirect constraints. It affects how much you can spend on various infrastructure, data, and software. For example, if you have low trading capital, your online brokerage will not be likely to supply you with real-time market data for too many stocks, so you can't really have a strategy that requires real-time market data over a large universe of stocks. (You can, of course, subscribe to a third-party market data vendor, but then the extra cost may not be justifiable if your trading capital is low.) Similarly, clean historical stock data with high frequency costs more than historical daily stock data, so a high-frequency stock-trading strategy may not be feasible with small capital expenditure. For historical stock data, there is another quality that may be even more important than their frequencies: whether the data are free of survivorship bias. I will define survivorship bias in the following section. Here, we just need to know that historical stock data without survivorship bias are much more expensive than those that have such a bias. Yet if your data have survivorship bias, the backtest result can be unreliable.

The same consideration applies to news—whether you can afford a high-coverage, real-time news source such as Bloomberg determines whether a news-driven strategy is a viable one. Same for fundamental (i.e., companies' financial) data—whether you can afford a good historical database with fundamental data on companies determines whether you can build a strategy that relies on such data.

Table 2.2 lists how capital (whether for trading or expenditure) constraint can influence your many choices.

This table is, of course, not a set of hard-and-fast rules, just some issues to consider. For example, if you have low capital but opened an account at a proprietary trading firm, then you will be free of many of the considerations above (though not expenditure on infrastructure). I started my life as an independent quantitative trader with $100,000 at a retail brokerage account (I chose Interactive Brokers), and I traded only directional, intraday stock strategies at first. But when I developed a strategy that sometimes requires much more leverage in order to be profitable, I signed up as a member of a proprietary trading firm as well. (Yes, you can have both, or more, accounts simultaneously. In fact, there are good reasons to do so if only for the sake of comparing their execution speeds and access to liquidity. See "Choosing a Brokerage or Proprietary Trading Firm" in Chapter 4.)

Despite my frequent admonitions here and elsewhere to beware of historical data with survivorship bias, when I first started I downloaded only the split-and-dividend-adjusted Yahoo! Finance data

TABLE 2.2 How Capital Availability Affects Your Many Choices

Low Capital	High Capital
Proprietary trading firm's membership	Retail brokerage account
Futures, currencies, options	Everything, including stocks
Intraday	Both intra- and interday (overnight)
Directional	Directional or market neutral
Small stock universe for intraday trading	Large stock universe for intraday trading
Daily historical data with survivorship bias	High-frequency historical data, survivorship bias–free
Low-coverage or delayed news source	High-coverage, real-time news source
No historical news database	Survivorship bias–free historical news database
No historical fundamental data on stocks	Survivorship bias–free historical fundamental data on stocks

using the download program from HQuotes.com (more on the different databases and tools in Chapter 3). This database is not survivorship bias–free—but more than two years later, I am still using it for most of my backtesting! In fact, a trader I know, who each day trades more than 10 times my account size, typically uses such biased data for his backtesting, and yet his strategies are still profitable. How can this be possible? Probably because these are intraday strategies. It seems that the only people I know who are willing and able to afford survivorship bias–free data are those who work in money management firms trading tens of millions of dollars or more (that includes my former self). So, you see, as long as you are aware of the limitations of your tools and data, you can cut many corners and still succeed.

Though futures afford you high leverage, some futures contracts have such a large size that it would still be impossible for a small account to trade. For instance, though the platinum future contract on the New York Mercantile Exchange (NYMEX) has a margin requirement of only $8,100, its nominal value is currently about $100,000. Furthermore, its volatility is such that a 6 percent daily move is not too rare, which translates to a $6,000 daily profit-and-loss (P&L) swing in your account due to just this one contract. (Believe me, I used to have a few of these contracts in my account, and it is a sickening feeling when they move against you.) In contrast, ES, the E-mini S&P 500 future on the Chicago Mercantile Exchange (CME, soon to be merged with NYMEX), has a nominal value of about $67,500, and a 6 percent or larger daily move happened only twice in the last 15 years. That's why its margin requirement is $4,500, only 55 percent that of the platinum contract.

Your Goal

Most people who choose to become traders want to earn a steady (hopefully increasing) monthly, or at least quarterly, income. But you may be independently wealthy, and long-term capital gain is all that matters to you. The strategies to pursue for short-term income versus long-term capital gain are distinguished mainly by their holding periods. Obviously, if you hold a stock for an average of one year, you won't be generating much monthly income (unless you started trading a while ago and have launched a new subportfolio every month, which you proceed to hold for a year—that is, you stagger your portfolios.) More subtly, even if your strategy holds a stock only for a month on average, your month-to-month profit fluctuation is likely to be fairly large (unless you hold hundreds of different stocks in your portfolio, which can be a result of staggering your portfolios), and therefore you cannot count on generating income on a monthly basis. This relationship between holding period (or, conversely, the trading frequency) and consistency of returns (that is, the Sharpe ratio or, conversely, the drawdown) will be discussed further in the following section. The upshot here is that the more regularly you want to realize profits and generate income, the shorter your holding period should be.

There is a misconception aired by some investment advisers, though, that if your goal is to achieve maximum long-term capital growth, then the best strategy is a buy-and-hold one. This notion has been shown to be mathematically false. In reality, maximum long-term growth is achieved by finding a strategy with the maximum Sharpe ratio (defined in the next section), *provided that you have access to sufficiently high leverage.* Therefore, comparing a short-term strategy with a very short holding period, small annual return, but very high Sharpe ratio, to a long-term strategy with a long holding period, high annual return, but lower Sharpe ratio, it is still preferable to choose the short-term strategy even if your goal is long-term growth, barring tax considerations and the limitation on your margin borrowing (more on this surprising fact later in Chapter 6 on money and risk management).

A TASTE FOR PLAUSIBLE STRATEGIES AND THEIR PITFALLS

Now, let's suppose that you have read about several potential strategies that fit your personal requirements. Presumably, someone else has done backtests on these strategies and reported that they have great historical returns. Before proceeding to devote your time to performing a comprehensive backtest on this strategy (not to mention devoting your capital to actually trading this strategy), there are a number of quick checks you can do to make sure you won't be wasting your time or money.

How Does It Compare with a Benchmark and How Consistent Are Its Returns?

This point seems obvious when the strategy in question is a stock-trading strategy that buys (but not shorts) stocks. Everybody seems to know that if a long-only strategy returns 10 percent a year, it is not too fantastic because investing in an index fund will generate as much, if not better, return on average. However, if the strategy is a long-short dollar-neutral strategy (i.e., the portfolio holds long and short positions with equal capital), then 10 percent is quite a good return, because then the benchmark of comparison is not the market index, but a riskless asset such as the yield of the three-month U.S. Treasury bill (which at the time of this writing is about 4 percent).

Another issue to consider is the consistency of the returns generated by a strategy. Though a strategy may have the same average return as the benchmark, perhaps it delivered positive returns every month while the benchmark occasionally suffered some very bad months. In this case, we would still deem the strategy superior. This leads us to consider the *information ratio* or *Sharpe ratio* (Sharpe, 1994), rather than returns, as the proper performance measurement of a quantitative trading strategy.

Information ratio is the measure to use when you want to assess a long-only strategy. It is defined as

$$\text{Information Ratio} = \frac{\text{Average of Excess Returns}}{\text{Standard Deviation of Excess Returns}}$$

where

$$\text{Excess Returns} = \text{Portfolio Returns} - \text{Benchmark Returns}$$

Now the benchmark is usually the market index to which the securities you are trading belong. For example, if you trade only small-cap stocks, the market index should be the Standard & Poor's small-cap index or the Russell 2000 index, rather than the S&P 500. If you are trading just gold futures, then the market index should be gold spot price, rather than a stock index.

The Sharpe ratio is actually a special case of the information ratio, suitable when we have a dollar-neutral strategy, so that the benchmark to use is always the risk-free rate. In practice, most traders use the Sharpe ratio even when they are trading a directional (long or short only) strategy, simply because it facilitates comparison across different strategies. Everyone agrees on what the risk-free rate is, but each trader can use a different market index to come up with their own favorite information ratio, rendering comparison difficult.

(Actually, there are some subtleties in calculating the Sharpe ratio related to whether and how to subtract the risk-free rate, how to annualize your Sharpe ratio for ease of comparison, and so on. I will cover these subtleties in the next chapter, which will also contain an example on how to compute the Sharpe ratio for a dollar-neutral and a long-only strategy.)

If the Sharpe ratio is such a nice performance measure across different strategies, you may wonder why it is not quoted more often instead of returns. In fact, when a colleague and I went to SAC Capital Advisors (assets under management: $14 billion) to pitch a strategy, their then head of risk management said to us: "Well, a high Sharpe ratio is certainly nice, but if you can get a higher return instead, we can all go buy bigger houses with our bonuses!" This reasoning is quite wrong: A higher Sharpe ratio will actually allow you to make more profits in the end, since it allows you to trade at a higher leverage. It is the leveraged return that matters in the end, not the nominal return of a trading strategy. For more on this, see Chapter 6 on money and risk management.

(And no, our pitching to SAC was not successful, but for reasons quite unrelated to the returns of the strategy. In any case, at that time neither my colleague nor I were familiar enough with the mathematical connection between the Sharpe ratio and leveraged returns to make a proper counterargument to that head of risk management.)

Now that you know what a Sharpe ratio is, you may want to find out what kind of Sharpe ratio your candidate strategies have. Often, they are not reported by the authors of that strategy, and you will have to e-mail them in private for this detail. And often, they will oblige, especially if the authors are finance professors; but if they refuse, you have no choice but to perform the backtest yourself. Sometimes, however, you can still make an educated guess based on the flimsiest of information:

- If a strategy trades only a few times a year, chances are its Sharpe ratio won't be high. This does not prevent it from being part of your multistrategy trading business, but it does disqualify the strategy from being your main profit center.
- If a strategy has deep (e.g., more than 10 percent) or lengthy (e.g., four or more months) drawdowns, it is unlikely that it will have a high Sharpe ratio. I will explain the concept of drawdown in the next section, but you can just visually inspect the equity curve (which is also the cumulative profit-and-loss curve, assuming no redemption or cash infusion) to see if it is very bumpy or not. Any peak-to-trough of that curve is a drawdown. (See Figure 2.1 for an example.)

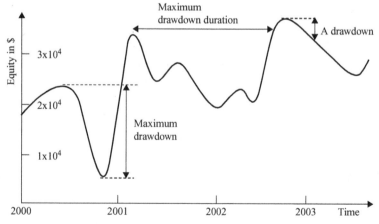

FIGURE 2.1 Drawdown, Maximum Drawdown, and Maximum Drawdown Duration

As a rule of thumb, any strategy that has a Sharpe ratio of less than 1 is not suitable as a stand-alone strategy. For a strategy that achieves profitability almost every month, its (annualized) Sharpe ratio is typically greater than 2. For a strategy that is profitable almost every day, its Sharpe ratio is usually greater than 3. I will show you how to calculate Sharpe ratios for various strategies in Examples 3.4, 3.6, and 3.7 in the next chapter.

How Deep and Long Is the Drawdown?

A strategy suffers a drawdown whenever it has lost money recently. A drawdown at a given time t is defined as the difference between the current equity value (assuming no redemption or cash infusion) of the portfolio and the global maximum of the equity curve occurring on or before time t. The *maximum drawdown* is the difference between the global maximum of the equity curve with the global minimum of the curve after the occurrence of the global maximum (time order matters here: The global minimum must occur later than the global maximum). The global maximum is called the "high watermark." The *maximum drawdown duration* is the longest it has taken for the equity curve to recover losses.

More often, drawdowns are measured in percentage terms, with the denominator being the equity at the high watermark, and the numerator being the loss of equity since reaching the high watermark.

Figure 2.1 illustrates a typical drawdown, the maximum drawdown, and the maximum drawdown duration of an equity curve. I will include a tutorial in Example 3.5 on how to compute these quantities from a table of daily profits and losses using either Excel or MATLAB. One thing to keep in mind: The maximum drawdown and the maximum drawdown duration do not typically overlap over the same period.

Defined mathematically, drawdown seems abstract and remote. However, in real life there is nothing more gut-wrenching and emotionally disturbing to suffer than a drawdown if you're a trader. (This is as true for independent traders as for institutional ones. When an institutional trading group is suffering a drawdown, everybody seems to feel that life has lost meaning and spend their days dreading the eventual shutdown of the strategy or maybe even the group as a whole.) It is therefore something we would want to minimize. You have to ask yourself, realistically, how deep and how long a drawdown will you be able to tolerate and not liquidate your portfolio and shut down your strategy? Would it be 20 percent and three months, or 10 percent and one month? Comparing your tolerance with the numbers obtained from the backtest of a candidate strategy determines whether that strategy is for you.

Even if the author of the strategy you read about did not publish the precise numbers for drawdowns, you should still be able to make an estimate from a graph of its equity curve. For example, in Figure 2.1, you can see that the longest drawdown goes from around February 2001 to around October 2002. So the maximum drawdown duration is about 20 months. Also, at the beginning of the maximum drawdown, the equity was about 2.3×10^4, and at the end, about 0.5×10^4. So the maximum drawdown is about 1.8×10^4.

How Will Transaction Costs Affect the Strategy?

Every time a strategy buys and sells a security, it incurs a transaction cost. The more frequent it trades, the larger the impact of transaction costs will be on the profitability of the strategy. These transaction costs are not just due to commission fees charged by the broker. There will also be the cost of liquidity—when you buy and sell securities at their market prices, you are paying the bid-ask spread. If you buy and sell securities using limit orders, however, you avoid the liquidity costs but incur opportunity costs. This is because your limit orders may not be executed, and therefore you may miss out on the potential profits of your trade. Also, when you buy or sell a large chunk of securities, you will not be able to complete the transaction without impacting the prices at which this transaction is done. (Sometimes just displaying a bid to buy a large number of shares for a stock can move the prices higher without your having bought a single share yet!) This effect on the market prices due to your own order is called *market impact*, and it can contribute to a large part of the total transaction cost when the security is not very liquid.

Finally, there can be a delay between the time your program transmits an order to your brokerage and the time it is executed at the exchange, due to delays on the Internet or various software-related issues. This delay can cause a "slippage," the difference between the price that triggers the order and the execution price. Of course, this slippage can be of either sign, but on average it will be a cost rather than a gain to the trader. (If you find that it is a gain on average, you should change your program to deliberately delay the transmission of the order by a few seconds!)

Transaction costs vary widely for different kinds of securities. You can typically estimate it by taking half the average bid-ask spread of a security and then adding the commission if your order size is not much bigger than the average sizes of the best bid and offer. If you are trading S&P 500 stocks, for example, the average transaction cost (excluding commissions, which depend on your brokerage) would be about 5 basis points (that is, five-hundredths of a percent). Note that I count a round-trip transaction of a buy and then a sell as two transactions—hence, a round trip will cost 10 basis points in this example. If you are trading ES, the E-mini S&P 500 futures, the transaction cost will be about 1 basis point. Sometimes the authors whose strategies you read about will disclose that they have included transaction costs in their backtest performance, but more often they will not. If they haven't, then you just to have to assume that the results are before transactions, and apply your own judgment to its validity.

As an example of the impact of transaction costs on a strategy, consider this simple mean-reverting strategy on ES. It is based on Bollinger bands: that is, every time the price exceeds plus or minus 2 moving standard deviations of its moving average, short or buy, respectively. Exit the position when the price reverts back to within 1 moving standard deviation of the moving average. If you allow yourself to enter and exit every five minutes, you will find that the Sharpe ratio is about 3 without transaction costs—very excellent indeed! Unfortunately, the Sharpe ratio is reduced to –3 if we subtract 1 basis point as transaction costs, making it a very unprofitable strategy.

For another example of the impact of transaction costs, see Example 3.7.

Does the Data Suffer from Survivorship Bias?

A historical database of stock prices that does not include stocks that have disappeared due to bankruptcies, delistings, mergers, or acquisitions suffer from the so-called survivorship bias, because only "survivors" of those often unpleasant events remain in the database. (The same term can be applied to mutual fund or hedge fund databases that do not include funds that went out of business.) Backtesting a strategy using data with survivorship bias can be dangerous because it may inflate the historical performance of the strategy. This is especially true if the strategy has a "value" bent; that is, it tends to buy stocks that are cheap. Some stocks were cheap because the companies were going bankrupt shortly. So if your strategy includes only those cases when the stocks were very cheap but eventually survived (and maybe prospered) and neglects those cases where the stocks finally did get delisted, the backtest performance will, of course, be much better than what a trader would actually have suffered at that time.

So when you read about a "buy on the cheap" strategy that has great performance, ask the author of that strategy whether it was tested on survivorship bias–free (sometimes called "point-in-time") data. If not, be skeptical of its results. (A toy strategy that illustrates this can be found in Example 3.3.)

How Did the Performance of the Strategy Change over the Years?

Most strategies performed much better 10 years ago than now, at least in a backtest. There weren't as many hedge funds running quantitative strategies then. Also, bid-ask spreads were much wider then: So if you assumed the transaction cost today was applicable throughout the backtest, the earlier period would have unrealistically high returns.

Survivorship bias in the data might also contribute to the good performance in the early period. The reason that survivorship bias mainly inflates the performance of an earlier period is that the further back we go in our backtest, the more missing stocks we will have. Since some of those stocks are missing because they went out of business, a long-only strategy would have looked better in the early period of the backtest than what the actual profit and loss (P&L) would have been at that time. Therefore, when judging the suitability of a strategy, one must pay particular attention to its performance in the most recent few years, and not be fooled by the overall performance, which inevitably includes some rosy numbers back in the old days.

Finally, "regime shifts" in the financial markets can mean that financial data from an earlier period simply cannot be fitted to the same model that is applicable today. Major regime shifts can occur because of changes in securities market regulation (such as decimalization of stock prices or the elimination of the short-sale rule, which I allude to in Chapter 5) or other macroeconomic events (such as the subprime mortgage meltdown).

This point may be hard to swallow for many statistically minded readers. Many of them may think that the more data there is, the more statistically robust the backtest should be. This is true only when the financial time series is generated by a stationary process. Unfortunately, financial time series is famously nonstationary, due to all of the reasons given earlier.

It is possible to incorporate such regime shifts into a sophisticated "super"-model (as I will discuss in Example 7.1), but it is much simpler if we just demand that our model deliver good performance on recent data.

Does the Strategy Suffer from Data-Snooping Bias?

If you build a trading strategy that has 100 parameters, it is very likely that you can optimize those parameters in such a way that the historical performance will look fantastic. It is also very likely that the future performance of this strategy will look nothing like its historical performance and will turn out to be very poor. By having so many parameters, you are probably fitting the model to historical accidents in the past that will not repeat themselves in the future. Actually, this so-called data-snooping bias is very hard to avoid even if you have just one or two parameters (such as entry and exit thresholds), and I will leave the discussion on how to minimize its impact to Chapter 3. But, in general, the more rules the strategy has, and the more parameters the model has, the more likely it is going to suffer data-snooping bias. Simple models are often the ones that will stand the test of time. (See the sidebar on my views on artificial intelligence and stock picking.)

ARTIFICIAL INTELLIGENCE AND STOCK PICKING*

There was an article in the *New York Times* a short while ago about a new hedge fund launched by Mr. Ray Kurzweil, a pioneer in the field of artificial intelligence. (Thanks to my fellow blogger, Yaser Anwar, who pointed it out to me.) According to Kurzweil, the stock-picking decisions in this fund are supposed to be made by machines that ". . . can observe billions of market transactions to see patterns we could never see" (quoted in Duhigg, 2006).

While I am certainly a believer in algorithmic trading, I have become a skeptic when it comes to trading based on "artificial intelligence."

At the risk of oversimplification, we can characterize artificial intelligence (AI) as trying to fit past data points into a function with many, many parameters. This is the case for some of the favorite tools of AI: neural networks, decision trees, and genetic algorithms. With many parameters, we can for sure capture small patterns that no human can see. But do these patterns persist? Or are they random noises that will never replay again? Experts in AI assure us that they have many safeguards against fitting the function to transient noise. And indeed, such tools have been very effective in consumer marketing and credit card fraud detection. Apparently, the patterns of consumers and thefts are quite consistent over time, allowing such AI algorithms to work even with a large number of parameters. However, from my experience, these safeguards work far less well in financial markets prediction, and overfitting to the noise in historical data remains a rampant problem. As a matter of fact, I have built financial predictive models based on many of these AI algorithms in the past. Every time a carefully constructed model that seems to work marvels in backtest came up, they inevitably performed miserably going forward. The main reason for this seems to be that the amount of statistically independent financial data is far more limited compared to the billions of independent consumer and credit transactions available. (You may think that there is a lot of tick-by-tick financial data to mine, but such data is serially correlated and far from independent.)

This is not to say that no methods based on AI will work in prediction. The ones that work for me are usually characterized by these properties:

- They are based on a sound econometric or rational basis, and not on random discovery of patterns.
- They have few parameters that need to be fitted to past data.
- They involve linear regression only, and not fitting to some esoteric nonlinear functions.
- They are conceptually simple.
- All optimizations must occur in a lookback moving window, involving no future unseen data. And the effect of this optimization must be continuously demonstrated using this future, unseen data.

Only when a trading model is constrained in such a manner do I dare to allow testing on my small, precious amount of historical data. Apparently, Occam's razor works not only in science, but in finance as well.

*This section was adapted from my blog article "Artificial Intelligence and Stock Picking," which you can find at epchan.blogspot.com/2006/12/artificial-intelligence-and-stock.html.

Does the Strategy "Fly under the Radar" of Institutional Money Managers?

Since this book is about starting a quantitative trading business from scratch, and not about starting a hedge fund that manages multiple millions of dollars, we should not be concerned whether a strategy is one that can absorb multiple millions of dollars. (*Capacity* is the technical term for how much a strategy can absorb without negatively impacting its returns.) In fact, quite the opposite—you should look for those strategies that fly under the radar of most institutional investors, for example, strategies that have very low capacities because they trade too often, strategies that trade very few stocks every day, or strategies that have very infrequent positions (such as some seasonal trades in commodity futures described in Chapter 7). Those niches are the ones that are likely still to be profitable because they have not yet been completely arbitraged away by the gigantic hedge funds.

SUMMARY

Finding prospective quantitative trading strategies is not difficult. There are:

- Business school and other economic research web sites.
- Financial web sites and blogs focusing on the retail investors.
- Trader forums where you can exchange ideas with fellow traders.

After you have done a sufficient amount of Net surfing or trading magazine riffling, you will find a number of promising trading strategies. Whittle them down to just a handful based on your personal circumstances and requirements, and by applying the screening criteria (more accurately described as healthy skepticism) that I listed earlier:

- How much time do you have for baby-sitting your trading programs?
- How good a programmer are you?
- How much capital do you have?
- Is your goal to earn steady monthly income or to strive for a large, long-term capital gain?

Even before doing an in-depth backtest of the strategy, you can quickly filter out some unsuitable strategies if they fail one or more of these tests:

- Does it outperform a benchmark?
- Does it have a high enough Sharpe ratio?
- Does it have a small enough drawdown and short enough drawdown duration?
- Does the backtest suffer from survivorship bias?
- Does the strategy lose steam in recent years compared to its earlier years?

- Does the strategy have its own "niche" that protects it from intense competition from large institutional money managers?

After making all these quick judgments, you are now ready to proceed to the next chapter, which is to rigorously backtest the strategy yourself to make sure that it does what it is advertised to do.

CHAPTER 3

Backtesting

A key difference between a traditional investment management process and a quantitative investment process is the possibility of backtesting a quantitative investment strategy to see how it would have performed in the past. Even if you found a strategy described in complete detail with all the historical performance data available, you would still need to backtest it yourself. This exercise serves several purposes. If nothing else, this replication of the research will ensure that you have understood the strategy completely and have reproduced it exactly for implementation as a trading system. Just as in any medical or scientific research, replicating others' results also ensures that the original research did not commit any of the common errors plaguing this process. But more than just performing due diligence, doing the backtest yourself allows you to experiment with variations of the original strategy, thereby refining and improving the strategy.

In this chapter, I will describe the common platforms that can be used for backtesting, various sources of historical data useful for backtesting, a minimal set of standard performance measures that a backtest should provide, common pitfalls to avoid, and simple refinements and improvements to strategies. A few fully developed backtesting examples will also be presented to illustrate the principles and techniques described.

COMMON BACKTESTING PLATFORMS

There are numerous commercial platforms that are designed for backtesting, some of them costing tens of thousands of dollars. In keeping with the focus on start-ups in this book, I start with those with which I am familiar and that can be purchased economically and are widely used.

Excel

This is the most basic and most common tool for traders, whether retail or institutional. You can enhance its power further if you can write Visual Basic macros. The beauty of Excel is "What you see is what you get" (or WYSIWYG in computing parlance). Data and program are all in one place so that nothing is hidden. Also, a common backtesting pitfall called "look-ahead bias," which will be explained later, is unlikely to occur in Excel (unless you use macros, which renders it no longer WYSIWYG) because you can easily align the dates with the various data columns and signals on a spreadsheet. Another advantage of Excel is that often backtesting and live trade generation can be done from the same spreadsheet, eliminating any duplication of programming efforts. The major disadvantage of Excel is that it can be used to backtest only fairly simple models. But, as I explained in the previous chapter, simple models are often the best!

MATLAB

MATLAB® (www.mathworks.com) is one of the most common backtesting platforms used by quantitative analysts and traders in large institutions. It is ideal for testing strategies that involve a large portfolio of stocks. (Imagine backtesting a strategy involving 1,500 symbols on Excel—it is possible, but quite painful.). It has numerous advanced statistical and mathematical modules built in, so traders do not have to reinvent the wheel if their trading algorithms involve some sophisticated but common mathematical concepts.

(A good example is principal component analysis—often used in factor models in statistical arbitrage trading, and a hassle to implement in other programming languages. See Example 7.4.) There is also a large number of third-party freeware available for download from the Internet, many of them very useful for quantitative trading purposes (an example is the cointegration package used in Example 7.2). Finally, MATLAB is very useful in retrieving web pages with financial information and parsing it into a useful form (so-called web scraping). Example 3.1 shows how this can be done.

Despite the seeming sophistication of the platform, it is actually very easy to learn (at least for basic usage) and it is very quick to write a complete backtest program using this language. The main drawback of MATLAB is that it is relatively expensive: it costs over $1,000 to acquire a license. However, there are several clones of MATLAB on the market where you can write and use codes that are very similar to MATLAB:

- O-Matrix (www.omatrix.com)
- Octave (www.gnu.org/software/octave)
- Scilab (www.scilab.org)

These clones may cost only several hundred dollars, or may be entirely free. Not surprisingly, the more expensive the clone is, the more compatible it is with programs written in MATLAB. (Of course, if you intend to write all the programs yourself and not use any third party's codes, compatibility is not an issue. But then you would be forfeiting one of the main benefits of using this language.) The other drawback of MATLAB is that it is very useful for backtesting but clumsy to use as an execution platform. So, often, you will need to build a separate execution system in another language once you have backtested your strategy. Despite these drawbacks, MATLAB has found widespread use within the quantitative trading community. I will include MATLAB codes for all the backtesting examples in this book as well as provide a quick survey of the MATLAB language itself in the appendix.

Example 3.1: Using MATLAB to Scrape Web Pages for Financial Data

MATLAB is not only useful for numerical computations, but also for text parsing. Following is an example of using MATLAB to retrieve a stock's historical price information from Yahoo! Finance:

```
clear; % make sure previously defined variables are
%erased.

symbol='IBM'; % the stock of interest
% retrieving a webpage
historicalPriceFile =...
urlread(['http://finance.yahoo.com/q/hp?s=', symbol]);

% extracting the date field to a cell array of cells
dateField=...
regexp(historicalPriceFile, ...
'<td class="yfnc_tabledata1" nowrap align="right">...
([\d\w-]+)</td>', 'tokens');

% extracting the numbers field to a cell array of cells
numField=regexp(historicalPriceFile, ...
'<td class="yfnc_tabledata1" align="right">...
([\d\.,]+)</td>', 'tokens');

% convert to cell array of strings
dates=[dateField{:}]';

% convert to cell array of strings
numField=[numField{:}]';

% convert to doubles array
op=str2double(numField (1:6:end)); % open
hi=str2double(numField (2:6:end)); % high
lo=str2double(numField (3:6:end)); % low
cl=str2double(numField (4:6:end)); % close
vol=str2double(numField (5:6:end)); % volume
adjCl=str2double(numField (6:6:end)); % adjusted close
```

This program file is available for download as epchan.com/book/example3_1.m, with "sharperatio" as both username and password. There is one limitation to this web-scraping script: It can retrieve only one web page at a time. Because Yahoo! displays its historical data over many pages, it is not really useful for retrieving the entire price history of IBM. Nevertheless, it is a simple illustration of MATLAB's text processing functions.

TradeStation

TradeStation (www.tradestation.com) is familiar to many retail traders as a brokerage that provides all-in-one backtesting and trade execution platforms linked to the brokerage's servers. The main advantages of this setup are:

- Most of the historical data necessary for backtesting is readily available, whereas you have to download the data from somewhere else if you use Excel or MATLAB.
- Once you have backtested the program, you can immediately generate orders using the same program and transmit them to the brokerage.

The disadvantages of this approach are that once you have written the software for your strategy, you are tied to TradeStation as your broker, and the proprietary language used by TradeStation is not as flexible as MATLAB and does not include some of the more advanced statistical and mathematical functions some traders use. Nevertheless, if you prefer the ease of use of an all-in-one system, TradeStation may be a good choice.

Since I have not used TradeStation in my own work, I will not include backtesting examples in TradeStation.

High-End Backtesting Platforms

In case you do have the financial resources to purchase a high-end, institutional-grade backtesting platform, here is a partial list:

- FactSet's Alpha Testing (www.factset.com/products/directions/qim/alphatesting)
- Clarifi's ModelStation (www.clarifi.com/ModelStation-Overview.php)
- Quantitative Analytics' MarketQA (www.qaisoftware.com)
- Barra's Aegis System (www.mscibarra.com/products/analytics/aegis)
- Logical Information Machines (www.lim.com)
- Alphacet's Discovery (www.alphacet.com)

Of all these, I have personal experience with only Logical Information Machines and Alphacet Discovery. Logical Information Machines is excellent for testing futures trading strategies, but it is weaker for equities strategies, based on my experience 10 years ago. Alphacet Discovery is a new product that integrates data retrieval, backtesting, optimization with machine learning algorithms, and automated execution. It is quite powerful for backtesting and trading a range of markets including futures, equities, and currencies. Example 7.1 is a backtest example using the Discovery platform.

FINDING AND USING HISTORICAL DATABASES

If you have a strategy in mind that requires a specific type of historical data, the first thing to do is to Google that type of data. You will be surprised how many free or low-cost historical databases are available out there for many types of data. (For example, try the search phrase "free historical intraday futures data.") Table 3.1 includes a number of the databases that I have found useful over the years, most of them either free or very low cost. I have deliberately left out the expensive databases from Bloomberg, Dow Jones, FactSet, Thomson Reuters, or Tick Data. Though they have almost every type of data imaginable for purchase, these data vendors cater mostly to more established institutions and are typically not in the price range of individuals or start-up institutions.

While finding sources of data on the Internet is even easier than finding prospective strategies, there are a number of issues and pitfalls with many of these databases that I will discuss later in this section. These issues apply mostly to stock and exchange-traded fund (ETF) data only. Here are the most important ones.

Are the Data Split and Dividend Adjusted?

When a company had its stocks split N to 1 (N is usually 2, but can be a fraction like 0.5 as well. When N is smaller than 1, it is

TABLE 3.1 Historical Databases for Backtesting

Source	Pros	Cons
Daily Stock Data		
Finance.yahoo.com	Free. Split/dividend adjusted.	Has survivorship bias. Can download only one symbol at a time.
HQuotes.com	Low cost. Same data as finance.yahoo.com. Software enables download of multiple symbols.	Has survivorship bias. Split but not dividend adjusted.
CSIdata.com	Low cost. Source of Yahoo! and Google's historical data. Software enables download of multiple symbols.	Has survivorship bias.
TrackData.com	Low cost. Split/dividend adjusted. Software enables download of multiple symbols. Fundamental data available.	Has survivorship bias.
CRSP.com	Survivorship bias free.	Expensive. Updated only once a month.
Daily Futures Data		
Quotes-plus.com	Low cost. Software enables download of multiple symbols.	
CSIdata.com	(See above.)	
Daily Forex Data		
Oanda.com	Free.	
Intraday Stock Data		
HQuotes.com	(See above.)	Short history for intraday data.
Intraday Futures Data		
DTN.com	Bid-ask data history available as part of NxCore product.	Expensive: requires subscription to live datafeed.
Intraday Forex Data		
GainCapital.com	Free. Long history.	

called a *reverse split*) with an ex-date of T, all the prices before T need to be multiplied by $1/N$. Similarly, when a company issued a dividend $\$d$ per share with an ex-date of T, all the prices before T need to be multiplied by the number $(\text{Close}(T - 1) - d)/\text{Close}(T - 1)$, where $\text{Close}(T - 1)$ is the closing price of the trading day before T. Notice that I adjust the historical prices by a multiplier instead of subtracting $\$d$ so that the historical daily returns will remain the same pre- and postadjustment. This is the way Yahoo! Finance adjusts its historical data, and is the most common way. (If you adjust by subtracting $\$d$ instead, the historical daily changes in prices will be the same pre- and postadjustment, but not the daily returns.) If the historical data are not adjusted, you will find a drop in price at the ex-date's market open from previous day's close (apart from normal market fluctuation), which may trigger an erroneous trading signal.

I recommend getting historical data that are already split and dividend adjusted, because otherwise you would have to find a separate historical database (such as earnings.com) of splits and dividends and apply the adjustments yourself—a somewhat tedious and error-prone task, which I will describe in the following example.

Example 3.2: Adjusting for Splits and Dividends

Here we look at IGE, an ETF that has had both splits and dividends in its history. It had a 2:1 split on June 9, 2005 (the ex-date). Let's look at the unadjusted prices around that date (you can download the historical prices of IGE from Yahoo! Finance into an Excel spreadsheet):

Date	Open	High	Low	Close
6/10/2005	73.98	74.08	73.31	74
6/9/2005	72.45	73.74	72.23	73.74
6/8/2005	144.13	146.44	143.75	144.48
6/7/2005	145	146.07	144.11	144.11

We need to adjust the prices prior to 6/9/2005 due to this split. This is easy: $N = 2$ here, and all we need to do is to multiply those prices by $\frac{1}{2}$. The following table shows the adjusted prices:

Date	Open	High	Low	Close
6/10/2005	73.98	74.08	73.31	74
6/9/2005	72.45	73.74	72.23	73.74
6/8/2005	72.065	73.22	71.875	72.24
6/7/2005	72.5	73.035	72.055	72.055

Now, the astute reader will notice that the adjusted close prices here do not match the adjusted close prices displayed in the Yahoo! Finance table. The reason for this is that there have been dividends distributed after 6/9/2005, so the Yahoo! prices have been adjusted for all those as well. Since each adjustment is a multiplier, the aggregate adjustment is just the product of all the individual multipliers. Here are the dividends from 6/9/2005 to November 2007, together with the unadjusted closing prices of the previous trading days and the resulting individual multipliers:

Ex-Date	Dividend	Prev Close	Multiplier
9/26/2007	0.177	128.08	0.998618
6/29/2007	0.3	119.44	0.997488
12/21/2006	0.322	102.61	0.996862
9/27/2006	0.258	91.53	0.997181
6/23/2006	0.32	92.2	0.996529
3/27/2006	0.253	94.79	0.997331
12/23/2005	0.236	89.87	0.997374
9/26/2005	0.184	89	0.997933
6/21/2005	0.217	77.9	0.997214

(Check out the multipliers yourself on Excel using the formula I gave above to see if they agree with my values here.) So the aggregate multiplier for the dividends is simply $0.998618 \times 0.997488 \times \cdots \times 0.997214 = 0.976773$. This multiplier should be applied to all the unadjusted prices on or after 6/9/2005. The aggregate multiplier for the dividends and the split is $0.976773 \times 0.5 = 0.488386$, which should be applied to all the unadjusted prices before 6/9/2005. So let's look at the resulting adjusted prices after applying these multipliers:

Date	Open	High	Low	Close
6/10/2005	72.26163	72.35931	71.6072	72.28117
6/9/2005	70.76717	72.02721	70.55228	72.02721
6/8/2005	70.39111	71.51929	70.20553	70.56205
6/7/2005	70.81601	71.33858	70.38135	70.38135

Now compare with the table from Yahoo! around November 1, 2007:

Date	Open	High	Low	Close	Volume	Adj Close
6/10/2005	73.98	74.08	73.31	74	179300	72.28
6/9/2005	72.45	73.74	72.23	73.74	853200	72.03
6/8/2005	144.13	146.44	143.75	144.48	109600	70.56
6/7/2005	145	146.07	144.11	144.11	58000	70.38

You can see that the adjusted closing prices from our calculations and from Yahoo! are the same (after rounding to two decimal places). But, of course, when you are reading this, IGE will likely have distributed more dividends and may have even split further, so your Yahoo! table won't look like the one above. It is a good exercise to check that you can make further adjustments based on those dividends and splits that result in the same adjusted prices as your current Yahoo! table.

Are the Data Survivorship Bias Free?

We already covered this issue in Chapter 2. Unfortunately, databases that are free from survivorship bias are quite expensive and may not be affordable for a start-up business. One way to overcome this problem is to start collecting point-in-time data yourself for the benefit of your future backtest. If you save the prices each day of all the stocks in your universe to a file, then you will have a point-in-time or survivorship-bias-free database to use in the future. Another way to lessen the impact of survivorship bias is to backtest your strategies on more recent data so that the results are not distorted by too many missing stocks.

Here is a toy "buy low-price stocks" strategy (*Warning:* This toy strategy is hazardous to your financial health!). Let's say from a universe of the 1,000 largest stocks (based on market capitalization), we pick 10 that have the lowest closing prices at the beginning of the year and hold them (with equal initial capital) for one year. Let's look at what we would have picked if we had a good, survivorship-bias-free database:

SYMBOL	Closing Price on 1/2/2001	Closing Price on 1/2/2002	Terminal Price
ETYS	0.2188	NaN	0.125
MDM	0.3125	0.49	0.49
INTW	0.4063	NaN	0.11
FDHG	0.5	NaN	0.33
OGNC	0.6875	NaN	0.2
MPLX	0.7188	NaN	0.8
GTS	0.75	NaN	0.35
BUYX	0.75	NaN	0.17
PSIX	0.75	NaN	0.2188

All but MDM were delisted sometime between 1/2/2001 and 1/2/2002 (after all, the dot-com bubble was seriously bursting then!). The NaNs indicate those with nonexistent closing prices on 1/2/2002. The Terminal Price column indicates the last prices at which the stocks were traded on or before 1/2/2002. The total return on this portfolio in that year was –42 percent.

Now, let's look at what we would have picked if our database had survivorship bias and actually missed all those stocks that were delisted that year. We would then have picked the following list instead:

SYMBOL	Closing Price on 1/2/2001	Closing Price on 1/2/2002
MDM	0.3125	0.49
ENGA	0.8438	0.44
NEOF	0.875	27.9
ENP	0.875	0.05
MVL	0.9583	2.5
URBN	1.0156	3.0688
FNV	1.0625	0.81
APT	1.125	0.88
FLIR	1.2813	9.475
RAZF	1.3438	0.25

41

Notice that since we select only those stocks that "survived" until at least 1/2/2002, they all have closing prices on that day. The total return on this portfolio was 388 percent!

In this example, –42 percent was the actual return a trader would experience following this strategy, whereas 388 percent is a fictitious return that was due to survivorship bias in our database.

Does Your Strategy Use High and Low Data?

For almost all daily stock data, the high and low prices are far noisier than the open and close prices. What this means is that even when you had placed a buy limit order below the recorded high of a day, it might not have been filled, and vice versa for a sell limit order. (This could be due to the fact that a very small order was transacted at the high, or the execution could have occurred on a market to which your order was not routed. Sometimes, the high or low is simply due to an incorrectly reported tick that was not filtered out.) Hence, a backtest that relies on high and low data is less reliable than one that relies on the open and close.

Actually, sometimes even a market on open (MOO) or market on close (MOC) order might not be filled at the historical open and close prices shown in your data. This is due to the fact that the historical prices shown may be due to the primary exchange (e.g., New York Stock Exchange [NYSE]), or it may be a composite price including all the regional exchanges. Depending on where your order was routed, it may be filled at a different price from the historical opening or closing price shown in your dataset. Nevertheless, the discrepancies of the open and close prices usually have less impact on backtest performance than the errors in the high and low prices, since the latter almost always inflate your backtest returns.

After retrieving the data from a database, it is often advisable to do a quick error check. The simplest way to do this is to calculate the daily returns based on the data. If you have open, high, low, and close prices, you can calculate the various combinations of daily returns such as from the previous high to today's close as well. You can then examine closely those days with returns that are, say, 4 standard deviations away from the average. Typically, an extreme return should be accompanied by a news announcement, or should occur on a day when the market index also experienced extreme returns. If not, then your data is suspect.

PERFORMANCE MEASUREMENT

Quantitative traders use a good variety of performance measures. Which set of numbers to use is sometimes a matter of personal preference, but with ease of comparisons across different strategies and traders in mind, I would argue that the Sharpe ratio and drawdowns are the two most important. Notice that I did not include average annualized returns, the measure most commonly quoted by investors, because if you use this measure, you have to tell people a number of things about what denominator you use to calculate returns. For example, in a long-short strategy, did you use just one side of capital or both sides in the denominator? Is the return a leveraged one (the denominator is based on account equity), or is it unleveraged (the denominator is based on market value of the portfolio)? If the equity or market value changes daily, do you use a moving average as the denominator, or just the value at the end of each day or each month? Most (but not all) of these problems associated with comparing returns can be avoided by quoting Sharpe ratio and drawdown instead as the standard performance measures.

I introduced the concepts of the Sharpe ratio, maximum drawdown, and maximum drawdown duration in Chapter 2. Here, I will just note a number of subtleties associated with calculating the Sharpe ratio, and give some computational examples in both Excel and MATLAB.

There is one subtlety that often confounds even seasoned portfolio managers when they calculate Sharpe ratios: should we or shouldn't we subtract the risk-free rate from the returns of a dollar-neutral portfolio? The answer is no. A dollar-neutral portfolio is self-financing, meaning the cash you get from selling short pays for the purchase of the long securities, so the financing cost (due to the spread between the credit and debit interest rates) is small and can be neglected for many backtesting purposes. Meanwhile, the margin balance you have to maintain earns a credit interest close to the risk-free rate r_F. So let's say the strategy return (the portfolio return minus the contribution from the credit interest) is R, and the risk-free rate is r_F. Then the excess return used in calculating the Sharpe ratio is $R + r_F - r_F = R$. So, essentially, you can ignore the risk-free rate in the whole calculation and just focus on the returns due to your stock positions.

Similarly, if you have a long-only day-trading strategy that does not hold positions overnight, you again have no need to subtract the risk-free rate from the strategy return in order to obtain the excess returns, since you do not have financing costs in this case, either. In general, you need to subtract the risk-free rate from your strategy returns in calculating the Sharpe ratio only if your strategy incurs financing cost.

To further facilitate comparison across strategies, most traders annualize the Sharpe ratio. Most people know how to annualize the average returns. For example, if you have been using monthly returns, then the average annual return is just 12 times the average monthly return.

However, annualizing the standard deviation of returns is a bit trickier. Here, based on the assumption that the monthly returns are serially uncorrelated (Sharpe, 1994), the annual standard deviation of returns is $\sqrt{12}$ times the monthly standard deviation. Hence, overall, the annualized Sharpe ratio would be $\sqrt{12}$ times the monthly Sharpe ratio.

In general, if you calculate your average and standard deviation of returns based on a certain trading period T, whether T is a month, a day, or an hour, and you want to annualize these quantities, you have to first find out how many such trading periods there are in a year (call it N_T). Then

$$\text{Annualized Sharpe Ratio} = \sqrt{N_T} \times \text{Sharpe Ratio Based on } T$$

For example, if your strategy holds positions only during the NYSE market hours (9:30–16:00 ET), and the average hourly returns is R, and the standard deviation of the hourly returns is s, then the annualized Sharpe ratio is $\sqrt{1638} \times R/s$. This is because $N_T = (252$ trading days$) \times (6.5$ trading hours per trading day$) = 1,638$. (A common mistake is to compute N_T as $252 \times 24 = 6,048$.)

Example 3.4: Calculating Sharpe Ratio for Long-Only Versus Market-Neutral Strategies

Let's calculate the Sharpe ratio of a trivial long-only strategy for IGE: buying and holding a share since the close of November 26, 2001, and selling it at close of November 14, 2007. Assume the average risk-free rate during this period is 4 percent per annum in this example. You can download the daily prices from Yahoo! Finance, specifying the date range desired, and store them as an Excel file (not the default comma-separated file), which you can call IGE.xls. The next steps can be done in either Excel or MATLAB:

Using Excel

1. The file should have columns A–G already from the download.
2. Sort all the columns in ascending order of Date (use the Data-Sort function, choose the "Expand the selection" radio button, and choose the "Ascending" as well as the "My data has Header row" radio buttons).
3. In cell H3, type "=(G3-G2)/G2". This is the daily return.
4. Double-clicking the little black dot at the lower right corner of the cell H3 will populate the entire column H with daily returns of IGE.
5. For clarity, you can type "Dailyret" in the header cell H1.
6. In cell I3, type "=H3-0.04/252", which is the excess daily return, assuming a 4 percent per annum risk-free rate and 252 trading days in a year.
7. Double-clicking the little black dot at the lower right corner of cell I3 will populate the entire column I with excess daily returns.
8. For clarity, type "Excess Dailyret" in the header cell I1.

9. In cell I1506 (the last row in the next column), type "=SQRT(252)*AVERAGE(I3:I1505)/STDEV(I3:I1505)".

10. The number displayed in cell I1505, which should be "0.789317538", is the Sharpe ratio of this buy-and-hold strategy.

The finished spreadsheet is available at my web site at epchan.com/book/example3_4.xls.

Using MATLAB

```
% make sure previously defined variables are erased.
clear;

% read a spreadsheet named "IGE.xls" into MATLAB.
[num, txt]=xlsread('IGE');

% the first column (starting from the second row)
% contains the trading days in format mm/dd/yyyy.
tday=txt(2:end, 1);

% convert the format into yyyymmdd.
tday=datestr(datenum(tday, 'mm/dd/yyyy'), 'yyyymmdd');
% convert the date strings first into cell arrays and
% then into numeric format.
tday=str2double(cellstr(tday));
% the last column contains the adjusted close prices.
cls=num(:, end);
% sort tday into ascending order.
[tday sortIndex]=sort(tday, 'ascend');
% sort cls into ascending order of dates.
cls=cls(sortIndex);
% daily returns
dailyret=(cls(2:end)-cls(1:end-1))./cls(1:end-1);
% excess daily returns assuming risk-free rate of 4%
% per annum and 252 trading days in a year
excessRet=dailyret - 0.04/252;
% the output should be 0.7893
sharpeRatio=sqrt(252)*mean(excessRet)/std(excessRet)
```

This MATLAB code is also available for download at my web site (epchan.com/book/example3_4.m).

Now let's calculate the Sharpe ratio of a long-short market-neutral strategy. In fact, it is a very trivial twist of the buy-and-hold strategy above: at the time we bought IGE, let's suppose we just shorted an equal dollar amount of Standard & Poor's depositary receipts (SPY) as a hedge, and closed both positions at the same time in November 2007. You can also download SPY from Yahoo! Finance and store it in a file SPY.xls. You can go through very similar steps as above in both Excel and MATLAB, and I will leave it as an exercise for the reader to perform the exact steps:

Using Excel

1. Sort the columns in SPY.xls in ascending order of date just like above.
2. Copy column G (Adj Close) in SPY.xls and paste it onto column J of IGE.xls above.
3. Check that column J has the same number of rows as columns A–I. If not, you have a different set of dates—make sure you download the matching date range from Yahoo!.
4. Perform the same steps as above to calculate the daily returns in column K.
5. For clarity, type "dailyretSPY" as the header in column K.
6. In column L, compute the net returns for the hedged strategy as the difference between column H and K divided by 2. (Divide by 2 because we now have twice the capital.)
7. In cell L1506, compute the Sharpe ratio of this hedged strategy. You should get "0.783681".

Using MATLAB

```
% Assume this is a continuation of the above MATLAB
%code.

% Insert your own code here to retrieve data from
% SPY.xls just as above.

% Name the array that contains the daily returns of
% SPY "dailyretSPY".

% net daily returns
(divide by 2 because we now have twice as much capital.)
netRet=(dailyret - dailyretSPY)/2;

% the output should be 0.7837.
sharpeRatio=sqrt(252)*mean(excessRet)/std(excessRet)
```

Example 3.5: Calculating Maximum Drawdown and Maximum Drawdown Duration

We shall continue the preceding long-short market-neutral example in order to illustrate the calculation of maximum drawdown and maximum drawdown duration. The first step in this calculation is to calculate the "high watermark" at the close of each day, which is the maximum cumulative return of the strategy up to that time. (Using the cumulative return curve to calculate high watermark and drawdown is equivalent to using the equity curve, since equity is nothing more than initial investment times 1 plus the cumulative return.) From the high watermark, we can calculate the drawdown, the maximum drawdown, and maximum drawdown duration.

Using Excel

1. In cell M3, type "=L3".
2. In cell M4, type "=(1+M3)*(1+L4)-1". This is the cumulative compounded return of the strategy up to that day. Populate the entire column M with the cumulative compounded returns of the strategy and erase the last cell of the column. Name this column Cumret.
3. In cell N3, type "=M3".
4. In cell N4, type "=MAX(N3, M4)". This is the high watermark up to that day. Populate the entire column N with the running high watermark of the strategy and erase the last cell of the column. Name this column High watermark.
5. In cell O3, type "=(1+N3)/(1+M3)-1". This is the drawdown at that day's close. Populate the entire column O with the drawdowns of the strategy.
6. In cell O1506, type "=MAX(O3:O1505)". This is the maximum drawdown of the strategy. It should have a value of about 0.1053, that is, a maximum drawdown of 10.53 percent.
7. In cell P3, type "=IF(O3=0, 0, P2+1)". This is the duration of the current drawdown. Populate the entire column R with the drawdown durations of the strategy and erase the last cell of the column.
8. In cell P1506, type "=MAX(P3:P1505)". This is the maximum drawdown duration of the strategy. It should have a value of 497, that is, a maximum drawdown duration of 497 trading days.

Using MATLAB

```
% Assume this is a continuation of the above MATLAB
% code.
% cumulative compounded returns
```

```
cumret=cumprod(1+netRet)-1;plot(cumret);

[maxDrawdown maxDrawdownDuration]=...
calculateMaxDD(cumret);

  [maxDrawdown maxDrawdownDuration]=...
calculateMaxDD(cumret);

% maximum drawdown. Output should be 0.1053
maxDrawdown
% maximum drawdown duration. Output should be 497.
maxDrawdownDuration
```

Notice the code fragment above calls a function "calculateMaxDrawdown," which I display below.

```
function [maxDD maxDDD]=calculateMaxDD(cumret)
% [maxDD maxDDD]=calculateMaxDD(cumret)
% calculation of maximum drawdown and maximum drawdown
% duration based on cumulative compounded returns.

% initialize high watermarks to zero.
highwatermark=zeros(size(cumret));
% initialize drawdowns to zero.
drawdown=zeros(size(cumret));
% initialize drawdown duration to zero.
drawdownduration=zeros(size(cumret));
for t=2:length(cumret)
    highwatermark(t)=...
max(highwatermark(t-1), cumret(t));
    % drawdown on each day
  drawdown(t)=(1+highwatermark(t))/(1+cumret(t))-1;
    if (drawdown(t)==0)
        drawdownduration(t)=0;
    else
        drawdownduration(t)=drawdownduration(t-1)+1;
    end
end

maxDD=max(drawdown); % maximum drawdown

% maximum drawdown duration
maxDDD=max(drawdownduration);
```

The file that contains this function is available as epchan.com/book/ calculateMaxDD.m. You can see where the maximum drawdown and

maximum drawdown duration occurred in this plot of the cumulative returns in Figure 3.1.

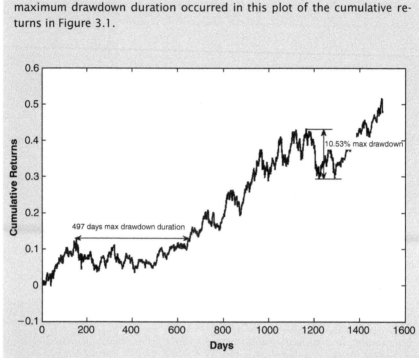

FIGURE 3.1 Maximum drawdown and maximum drawdown duration for
Example 3.4

COMMON BACKTESTING PITFALLS TO AVOID

Backtesting is the process of creating the historical trades given the
historical information available at that time, and then finding out
what the subsequent performance of those trades is. This process
seems easy given that the trades were made using a computer algorithm in our case, but there are numerous ways in which it can go
wrong. Usually, an erroneous backtest would produce a historical
performance that is better than what we would have obtained in actual trading. We have already seen how survivorship bias in the data
used for backtesting can result in inflated performance. There are,

however, other common pitfalls related to how the backtest program is written, or more fundamentally, to how you construct your trading strategy. I will describe two of the most common ones here, with tips on how to avoid them.

Look-Ahead Bias

This error refers to the situation when you are using information that was available only at a time *ahead* of the instant the trade was made. For example, if your trade entry rule reads: "Buy when the stock is within 1 percent of the day's low," you have introduced a look-ahead bias in your strategy, because you could not possibly have known what the day's low was until the market closed that day. Another example: Suppose a model involves a linear regression fit of two price series. If you use the regression coefficients obtained from the entire data set to determine your daily trading signals, you have again introduced look-ahead bias.

How do we avoid look-ahead bias? Use *lagged* historical data for calculating signals at every opportunity. Lagging a series of data means that you calculate all the quantities like moving averages, highs and lows, or even volume, based on data up to the close of the *previous* trading period only. (Of course, you needn't lag the data if your strategy enters only at the close of the period.)

Look-ahead bias is easier to avoid using Excel or other WYSIWYG programs than using MATLAB. This is because it is easy to align all the different columns of data in Excel and ensure that the formula in each cell is computed based on the rows above the current row. It would be visually obvious when one is using current day's data in generating signals, given the cell-highlighting functionality in Excel. (Double-clicking a cell with a formula will highlight the cells of data this formula utilizes.) With MATLAB, you have to be more careful and remember to run a lag function on certain series used for signal generation.

Even with all the care and caution that goes into creating a backtest program without look-ahead bias, sometimes we may still let some of it slip in. Some look-ahead bias is quite subtle in nature and not easy to avoid, especially if you are using MATLAB.

It is best to do a final checkup of your MATLAB backtest program using this method: Run the program using all your historical data; generate and save the resulting position file to file A (position file is the file that contains all the recommended positions generated by the program on each day). Now truncate your historical data so that the most recent portion (say N days) is removed. So if the last day in the original data is T, then the last day in the truncated data should be T-N. N could be 10 days to 100 days. Now run the back-test program again using the truncated data and save the resulting positions into a new file B. Truncate the most recent N rows of the positions file A so that both A and B have the same number of rows (days) in them, and the last day in both file A and B should be T-N. Finally, check if A and B are identical in their positions. If not, you have a look-ahead bias in your backtest program that you must find and correct, because the discrepancies in positions mean that you are inadvertently using the truncated part of the historical data (the part that lies ahead of day T-N) in determining the positions in file A. I will illustrate this somewhat convoluted procedure at the end of Example 3.6.

Data-Snooping Bias

In Chapter 2, I mentioned data-snooping bias—the danger that back-test performance is inflated relative to the future performance of the strategy because we have overoptimized the parameters of the model based on transient noise in the historical data. Data snoop-ing bias is pervasive in the business of predictive statistical models of historical data, but is especially serious in finance because of the limited amount of independent data we have. High-frequency data, while in abundant supply, is useful only for high-frequency models. And while we have stock market data stretching back to the early parts of the twentieth century, only data within the past 10 years are really suitable for building predictive model. Furthermore, as discussed in Chapter 2, regime shifts may render even data that are just a few years old obsolete for backtesting purposes. The less inde-pendent data you have, the fewer adjustable parameters you should employ in your trading model.

As a rule of thumb, I would not employ more than five parameters, including quantities such as entry and exit thresholds, holding period, or the lookback period, in computing moving averages. Furthermore, not all data-snooping bias is due to the optimization of parameters. Numerous choices one makes in creating a trading model can be affected by repeated backtesting on the same data set—decisions such as whether to enter at the open or close, whether to hold the positions overnight, whether to trade large-cap or mid-cap stocks. Often, these qualitative decisions are made to optimize the backtest performance, but they may not be optimal going forward. It is almost impossible to completely eliminate data-snooping bias as long as we are building data-driven models. However, there are ways to mitigate the bias.

Sample Size   The most basic safeguard against data-snooping bias is to ensure that you have a sufficient amount of backtest data relative to the number of free parameters you want to optimize. As a rule of thumb, let's assume that the number of data points needed for optimizing your parameters is equal to 252 times the number of free parameters your model has. (This assumption of proportionality is not based on any survey of the vast statistical literature, but purely on experience.) So, for example, let's assume you have a daily trading model with three parameters. Then you should have at least three years' worth of backtest data with daily prices. However, if you have a three-parameter trading model that updates positions every minute, then you should have at least 252/390 year, or about seven months, of one-minute backtest data. (Note that if you have a daily trading model, then even if you have seven months of minute-by-minute data points, effectively you only have about $7 \times 21 = 147$ data points, far from sufficient for testing a three-parameter model.)

Out-of-Sample Testing   Divide your historical data into two parts. Save the second (more recent) part of the data for out-of-sample testing. When you build the model, optimize the parameters as well as other qualitative decisions on the first portion (called the *training set*), but test the resulting model on the second portion (called the *test set*). (The two portions should be roughly equal in size, but if there is insufficient training data, we should at least have one-third as much test data as training data. The minimum size of the training set is determined by the rule of thumb in the previous section.) Ideally, the set of optimal parameters and decisions for the first part of the backtest period is also the optimal set for the second period, but things are rarely this perfect. The performance on the second part of the data should at least be reasonable. Otherwise, the model has data-snooping bias built into it, and one way to cure it is to simplify the model and eliminate some parameters.

A more rigorous (albeit more computationally intensive) method of out-of-sample testing is to use moving optimization of the parameters. In this case, the parameters themselves are constantly adapting to the changing historical data, and data-snooping bias with respect to parameters is eliminated. (See the sidebar on parameterless trading models.)

PARAMETERLESS TRADING MODELS*

A portfolio manager whom I used to work for liked to proudly proclaim that his trading models have "no free parameters." In keeping with the tradition of secrecy in our industry, he would not divulge his technique further.

Lately, I have begun to understand what a trading model with no free parameters means. It doesn't mean that it does not contain, for example, any lookback period for calculating trends, or thresholds for entry or exit. I think that would be impossible. It just means that all such parameters are *dynamically* optimized in a moving lookback window. This way, if you ask, "Does the model have a fixed profit cap?," the trader can honestly reply: "No, profit cap is not an input parameter. It is determined by the model itself."

The advantage of a parameterless trading model is that it minimizes the danger of overfitting the model to multiple input parameters (the so-called "data-snooping bias"). So the backtest performance should be much closer to the actual forward performance.

(Note that parameter optimization does not necessarily mean picking one *best* set of parameters that give the best backtest performance. Often, it is better to make a trading decision based on some kind of *averages* over different sets of parameters.)

Now, it is quite computationally challenging to optimize all these parameters just in time for your next order, but it is often even more difficult to do that in a backtest, given that a multidimensional optimization needs to be performed for each historical bar. As a result, I personally have seldom traded parameter-less models, until I get to research my regime-switching model described in Example 7.1. That model is almost parameterless (I left out a few parameters from optimization because of a lack of time, not because of any technical difficulties). How was I able to perform backtest parameter optimization within a few minutes in this case? I got to use a high-end backtesting platform (Alphacet Discovery).

*This section was adapted from my blog article "Parameterless Trading Models," which you can find at epchan.blogspot.com/2008/05/parameterless-trading-models.html.

The ultimate out-of-sample testing is familiar to many traders, and it is called *paper trading*. Running the model on actual unseen data is the most reliable way to test it (short of actually trading it). Paper trading not only allows you to perform a truly honest out-of-sample test; it often allows you to discover look-ahead errors in your programs, as well as making you aware of various operational issues. I will discuss paper trading in Chapter 5.

If the strategy that you are testing comes from a published source, and you are just conducting a backtest to verify that the results are correct, then the entire period between the time of publication and the time that you tested the strategy is a genuine out-of-sample period. As long as you do not optimize the parameters of the published model on the out-of-sample period, this period is as good as paper trading the strategy.

Example 3.6: Pair Trading of GLD and GDX

This example will illustrate how to separate the data into a training set and a test set. We will backtest a pair-trading strategy and optimize its parameters on the training set and look at the effect on the test set.

GLD versus GDX is a good candidate for pair trading because GLD reflects the spot price of gold, and GDX is a basket of gold-mining stocks. It makes intuitive sense that their prices should move in tandem. I have discussed this pair of ETFs extensively on my blog in connection with cointegration analysis (see, e.g., epchan.blogspot.com/2006/11/

reader-suggested-possible-trading.html). Here, however, I will defer until Chapter 7 the cointegration analysis on the training set, which demonstrates that the spread formed by long GLD and short GDX is mean reverting. Instead, we will perform a regression analysis on the training set to determine the hedge ratio between GLD and GDX, and then define entry and exit thresholds for a pair-trading strategy. We will see how optimizing these thresholds on the training set changes the performance on the test set. (This program is available as on epchan.com/book/example3_6.m. The data files are available as GDX.xls and GLD.xls. This program uses of a lag1 function will lag the time series by one time period. It is included at epchan.com/book as well. It also uses a function "ols" for linear regression, which is part of a free package downloaded from spatial-econometrics.com.)

Using MATLAB

```
% make sure previously defined variables are erased.
clear;
% read a spreadsheet named "GLD.xls" into MATLAB.
[num, txt]=xlsread('GLD');
% the first column (starting from the second row) is
% the trading days in format mm/dd/yyyy.
tday1=txt(2:end, 1);

% convert the format into yyyymmdd.
tday1=...
datestr(datenum(tday1, 'mm/dd/yyyy'), 'yyyymmdd');
% convert the date strings first into cell arrays and
% then into numeric format.
tday1=str2double(cellstr(tday1));
% the last column contains the adjusted close prices.
adjcls1=num(:, end);
% read a spreadsheet named "GDX.xls" into MATLAB.
[num, txt]=xlsread('GDX');
% the first column (starting from the second row) is
% the trading days in format mm/dd/yyyy.
tday2=txt(2:end, 1);
% convert the format into yyyymmdd.
tday2=...
datestr(datenum(tday2, 'mm/dd/yyyy'), 'yyyymmdd');

% convert the date strings first into cell arrays and
% then into numeric format.
tday2=str2double(cellstr(tday2));
```

```
% the last column contains the adjusted close prices.
adjcls2=num(:, end);

% find the intersection of the two data sets,
% and sort them in ascending order
[tday, idx1, idx2]=intersect(tday1, tday2);
cl1=adjcls1(idx1);
 cl2=adjcls2(idx2);

trainset=1:252; % define indices for training set

% define indices for test set
testset=trainset(end)+1:length(tday);
% determines the hedge ratio on the trainset
% use regression function
results=ols(cl1(trainset), cl2(trainset));
hedgeRatio=results.beta;

% spread = GLD - hedgeRatio*GDX
 spread=cl1-hedgeRatio*cl2;
plot(spread(trainset));

figure;

plot(spread(testset));

figure;

% mean  of spread on trainset
spreadMean=mean(spread(trainset));
% standard deviation of spread on trainset
spreadStd=std(spread(trainset));
% z-score of spread
zscore=(spread - spreadMean)./spreadStd;
% buy spread when its value drops below 2 standard
  deviations.
longs=zscore<=-2;

% short spread when its value rises above 2 standard
  deviations.
shorts=zscore>=2;
% exit any spread position when its value is within 1
% standard deviation of its mean.
exits=abs(zscore)<=1;
% initialize positions array
positions=NaN(length(tday), 2);
```

```
% long entries
positions(shorts, :)=...
repmat([-1 1], [length(find(shorts)) 1]);
% short entries
positions(longs,  :)=repmat([1 -1],
  [length(find(longs)) 1]);
% exit positions
positions(exits,  :)=zeros(length(find(exits)), 2);
% ensure existing positions are carried forward
  unless there is an exit signal positions=
  fillMissingData(positions);
cl=[cl1 cl2]; % combine the 2 price series

dailyret=(cl - lag1(cl))./lag1(cl);

pnl=sum(lag1(positions).*dailyret, 2);

% the Sharpe ratio on the train-
ing set should be about 2.3
sharpeTrainset=...
sqrt(252)*mean(pnl(trainset(2:end))).
  /std(pnl(trainset(2:end)))


% the Sharpe ratio on the test set should be about 1.5
sharpeTestset=sqrt(252)*mean(pnl(testset)).
/std(pnl(testset))
plot(cumsum(pnl(testset)));
% save positions file for checking look-ahead bias.
save example3_6_positions positions;
```

In file lag1.m:

```
function y=lag1(x)
% y=lag(x)
if (isnumeric(x))
    % populate the first entry with NaN
  y=[NaN(1,size(x,2));x(1:end-1, :)];elseif (ischar(x))
    % populate the first entry with "
y=[repmat(",[1 size(x,2)]);x(1:end-1, :)];else
    error('Can only be numeric or char array');
end
```

So this pair-trading strategy has excellent Sharpe ratios on both the training set and the test set. Therefore, this strategy can be considered free of data-snooping bias. However, there may be room for improvement. Let's see what happens if we change the entry thresholds to 1 standard deviation and exit threshold to 0.5 standard deviation. In this case, the Sharpe ratio on the training set increases to 2.9 and the Sharpe ratio on the test set increases to 2.1. So, clearly, this set of thresholds is better.

Often, however, optimizing the parameters on the training set may decrease the performance on the test set. In this situation, you should choose a set of parameters that result in good (but may not be the best) performance on both training and test sets.

I have not incorporated transaction costs (which I discuss in the next section) into this analysis. You can try to add that as an exercise. Since this strategy doesn't trade very frequently, transaction costs do not have a big impact on the resulting Sharpe ratio.

To see why this strategy works, just take a look at the Figure 7.4 of the spread, which I will discuss in connection with stationarity and cointegration in Chapter 7. You can see that the spread behaves in a highly mean-reverting manner. Hence, buying low and selling high over and over again works well here.

One last check, though, that we should perform before calling this a success: We need to check for any look-ahead bias in the backtest program. Add the following code fragment to the MATLAB code above after the line "cl2=adjcls2(idx2);"

```
% number of most recent trading days to cut off
cutoff=60;% remove the last cutoff number of days.
tday(end-cutoff+1:end, :)=[];
cl1(end-cutoff+1:end, :)=[];
cl2(end-cutoff+1:end, :)=[];
```

Add the following code fragment to the very end of the previous MATLAB program, replacing the line "save example3_6_positions positions".

```
% step two of look-forward-bias check
oldoutput=load('example3_6_positions');
oldoutput.positions(end-cutoff+1:end, :)=[];

if (any(positions~=oldoutput.positions))
    fprintf(1, 'Program has look-forward-bias!\n');
end
```

Save this new program into file "example3_6_1.m" and run it. You will find that the sentence "Program has look-forward-bias" is not printed out—this indicates that our algorithm passed our test.

Sensitivity Analysis Once you have optimized your parameters as well as various features of your model and have verified that its performance on a test set is still reasonable, vary these parameters or make some small qualitative changes in the features of the model and see how the performance changes on both the training and the test sets. If the drop is so drastic that any parameter set other than the optimal one is unacceptable, the model most likely suffers from data-snooping bias.

There are some variations on your model that are particularly important to try: the various ways to simplify the model. Do you really need, say, five different conditions to determine whether to make that trade? What if you eliminate the conditions one by one—at what point does the performance on the training set deteriorate to an unacceptable level? And more important: Is there a corresponding decrease in performance on the test set as you eliminate the conditions? In general, you should eliminate as many conditions, constraints, and parameters as possible as long as there is no significant decrease in performance in the test set, even though it may decrease performance on the training set. (But you should not add conditions and parameters, or adjust the parameter values, so as to improve performance on the test set: If you do, you have effectively used the test set as your training set and possibly reintroduce data-snooping bias to your model.)

When one has reduced the set of parameters and conditions that trigger a trade to the minimum, and after one has ascertained that small variations in these parameters and conditions do not drastically alter the out-of-sample performance, one should consider dividing the trading capital across the different parameter values and sets of conditions. This averaging over parameters will further help ensure that the actual trading performance of the model will not deviate too much from the backtest result.

TRANSACTION COSTS

No backtest performance is realistic without incorporating transaction costs. I discussed the various types of transactions costs (commission, liquidity cost, opportunity cost, market impact, and slippage) in Chapter 2 and have given examples of how to incorporate transaction costs into the backtest of a strategy. It should not surprise you to find that a strategy with a high Sharpe ratio before adding transaction costs can become very unprofitable after adding such costs. I will illustrate this in Example 3.7.

Example 3.7: A Simple Mean-Reverting Model with and without Transaction Costs

Here is a simple mean-reverting model that is due to Amir Khandani and Andrew Lo at MIT (available at web.mit.edu/alo/www/Papers/august07.pdf). This strategy is very simple: Buy the stocks with the worst previous one-day returns, and short the ones with the best previous one-day returns. Despite its utter simplicity, this strategy has had great performance since 1995, ignoring transaction costs (it has a Sharpe ratio of 4.47 in 2006). Our objective here is to find out what would happen to its performance in 2006 if we assume a standard 5-basis-point-per-trade transaction cost. (A *trade* is defined as a buy or a short, not a round-trip transaction.) This example strategy not only allows us to illustrate the impact of transaction costs, it also illustrates the power of MATLAB in backtesting a model that trades multiple securities—in other words, a typical statistical arbitrage model. Backtesting a model with a large number of symbols over multiple years is often too cumbersome to perform in Excel. But even assuming that you have MATLAB at your disposal, there is still the question of how to retrieve historical data for hundreds of symbols, especially survivorship-bias-free data. Here, we will put aside the question of survivorship bias because of the expensive nature of such data and just bear in mind that whatever performance estimates we obtained are upper bounds on the actual performance of the strategy.

Whenever one wants to backtest a stock selection strategy, the first question is always: Which universe of stocks? The typical starting point is the S&P 500 stock universe, which is the most liquid set of stocks available. The current list of stocks in the S&P 500 is available for download at the Standard & Poor's website (www.standardandpoors.com). Since the constituents of this universe change constantly, the list that you download will be different from mine. For ease of comparison, you can find my list saved as epchan.com/book/SP500_20071121.xls. The easiest way to download historical data for all these stocks is to buy a copy of the HQuote Pro software (referenced earlier in this chapter, available from HQuote.com.) This software conveniently allows you to cut and paste any list of symbols for which you want data. Run an update on your list in the software so as to retrieve the data from January 1, 2000, to the present day and then export this data to a single text file called "Export.txt," choosing only columns Date, Open, High, Low, Close, and Volume, without header. Now, use the following MATLAB program (epchan.com/book/retrieveHQuoteHistoricalPrice.m) to parse this data into a form useful for our computation, and which saves it to a binary file "SPX_20071123.mat" on your local directory:

```
clear;

inputFile='Export.txt';
outputFile='SPX_20071123';

[mysym, mytday, myop, myhi, mylo, mycl, myvol]=...
textread(inputFile, '%s %u %f %f %f %f %u', ...
'delimiter', ',');

% Since the single file consists of many symbols,
% we need to find the unique set of symbols.
stocks=unique(mysym);
% Since the single file consists of many repeating set
% of dates for different symbols, we need to find the
% unique set of dates.
tday=unique(mytday);


op=NaN(length(tday), length(stocks));
hi=NaN(length(tday), length(stocks));
lo=NaN(length(tday), length(stocks));
cl=NaN(length(tday), length(stocks));
vol=NaN(length(tday), length(stocks));


for s=1:length(stocks)
    stk=stocks{s};

    % find the locations (indices) of the data with
    % the current symbol.
idxA=strmatch(stk, mysym, 'exact');     % find the
   locations (indices) of the data with
 % the current set of dates.
  [foo, idxA, idxtB]=intersect(mytday(idxA), tday);

    % Extract the set of prices for the current symbol
```

```
% from the downloaded data.
   op(idxtB, s)=myop(idxA(idxtA));
   hi(idxtB, s)=myhi(idxA(idxtA));
   lo(idxtB, s)=mylo(idxA(idxtA));
   cl(idxtB, s)=mycl(idxA(idxtA));
   vol(idxtB, s)=myvol(idxA(idxtA));

end

save(outputFile, 'tday', 'stocks', 'op', 'hi', ...
'lo', 'cl', 'vol');
```

Next, we can use this historical data set to backtest the mean-reverting strategy without transaction cost:

```
clear;

startDate=20060101;
endDate=20061231;

load('SPX_20071123', 'tday', 'stocks', 'cl');

% daily returns
dailyret=(cl-lag1(cl))./lag1(cl);
% equal weighted market index return
marketDailyret=smartmean(dailyret, 2);
% weight of a stock is proportional to the negative
% distance to the market index.
weights=...
-(dailyret-repmat(marketDailyret,[1 size(dailyret,2)]))./
repmat(smartsum(isfinite(cl), 2), ...
[1 size(dailyret, 2)]);

% those stocks that do not have valid prices or
% daily returns are excluded.
weights(~isfinite(cl) | ~isfinite(lag1(cl)))=0;
dailypnl=smartsum(lag1(weights).*dailyret, 2);

% remove pnl outside of our dates of interest
dailypnl(tday < startDate | tday > endDate) = [];
% Sharpe ratio should be about 0.25
sharpe=...
sqrt(252)*smartmean(dailypnl, 1)/smartstd(dailypnl, 1)
```

This file was saved as epchan.com/book/example3_7.m on my web site. Notice that the Sharpe ratio in 2006 is only 0.25, not 4.47 as stated by the original authors. The reason for this drastically lower performance is due to the use of the large market capitalization universe of S&P 500 in our backtest. If you read the original paper by the authors, you will find that most of the returns are generated by small and microcap stocks.

In this MATLAB program, I have used three new functions: "smartsum," "smartmean," and "smartstd." They are very similar to the usual "sum," "mean," and "std" functions, except they skip all the NaN entries in the data. These functions are very useful in backtesting because price series for stocks often starts and stops. These files are all available at epchan.com/book.

```
function y = smartsum(x, dim)
%y = smartsum(x, dim)
%Sum along dimension dim, ignoring NaN.

hasData=isfinite(x);
x(~hasData)=0;
y=sum(x,dim);
y(all(~hasData, dim))=NaN;
```

"smartmean.m"

```
function y = smartmean(x, dim)
% y = smartmean(x, dim)
% Mean value along dimension dim, ignoring NaN.

hasData=isfinite(x);
x(~hasData)=0;
y=sum(x,dim)./sum(hasData, dim);
y(all(~hasData, dim))=NaN; % set y to NaN if all en-
tries are NaN's.
```

"smartstd.m"

```
function y = smartstd(x, dim)
%y = smartstd(x, dim)
% std along dimension dim, ignoring NaN and Inf

hasData=isfinite(x);
  x(~hasData)=0;
y=std(x);
y(all(~hasData, dim))=NaN;
```

Now, continuing with our backtest, let's see what happens if we deduct a 5-basis-point transaction cost for every trade.

```
% daily pnl with transaction costs deducted
onewaytcost=0.0005; % assume 5 basis points
```

```
% remove weights outside of our dates of interest
weights(tday < startDate | tday > endDate, :) = [];
% transaction costs are only incurred when
% the weights change
dailypnlminustcost=...
dailypnl - smartsum(abs(weights-lag1(weights)), 2).*
onewaytcost;

% Sharpe ratio should be about -3.19
sharpeminustcost=...
sqrt(252)*smartmean(dailypnlminustcost, 1)/...
smartstd(dailypnlminustcost, 1)
```

The strategy is now very unprofitable!

STRATEGY REFINEMENT

If a strategy does not deliver superb backtest performance on first trial, there are some common ways to improve it. How to refine a strategy without introducing data-snooping bias and to remain simple with few parameters is more of an art than a science. The guiding principle is the same as that of parameter optimization: Whatever changes you make to the strategy to improve its performance on the training set, it must also improve the performance on the test set.

Often, there are some very simple strategies that are fairly well known in traders' circles and are still somewhat profitable, though their returns seem to be diminishing. An example is the pair trading of stocks. The reason they are diminishing in returns is that too many traders are taking advantage of this arbitrage opportunity and gradually erasing the profit margin. However, it is often possible to introduce minor variations in the basic strategy, which will boost its returns.

These minor variations are often far less well known than the basic strategy, and therefore far less well exploited by traders. Sometimes they involve excluding certain stocks or groups of stocks from the universe. For example, traders often prefer to exclude pharmaceutical stocks from their technical trading program because of the dramatic impact of news on their prices, or else they may exclude stocks that have pending merger or acquisition deals. Other traders change the entry and exit timing or frequency of the trades. Yet another variation concerns the selection of the stock universe: We saw in Example 3.7 that a strategy that has a very good Sharpe ratio when it is applied to small-cap stocks becomes very unprofitable when applied to large-cap stocks.

When introducing these refinements to your strategy, it is preferable that the refinement has some basis in fundamental economics or a well-studied market phenomenon, rather than some arbitrary rule based on trial and error. Otherwise, data-snooping bias looms.

Example 3.8: A Small Variation on an Existing Strategy

Let's refine the mean-reverting strategy described above in Example 3.7. Recall that strategy has a mediocre Sharpe ratio of 0.25 and a very unprofitable Sharpe ratio of –3.19 after transaction costs in 2006. The only change we will make here is to update the positions at the market open instead of the close. In the MATLAB code, simply replace "cl" with "op" everywhere.

Lo and behold, the Sharpe ratio before costs increases to 4.43, and after costs, it increases to a profitable 0.78! I will leave it as an exercise for the reader to improve the Sharpe ratio further by testing the strategy on the S&P 400 mid-cap and S&P 600 small-cap universes.

SUMMARY

Backtesting is about conducting a realistic historical simulation of the performance of a strategy. The hope is that the future performance of the strategy will resemble its past performance, though as your investment manager will never tire of telling you, this is by no means guaranteed!

There are many nuts and bolts involved in creating a realistic historical backtest and in reducing the divergence of the future performance of the strategy from its backtest performance. Issues discussed here include:

- *Data:* Split/dividend adjustments, noise in daily high/low, and survivorship bias.
- *Performance measurement:* Annualized Sharpe ratio and maximum drawdown.
- *Look-ahead bias:* Using unobtainable future information for past trading decisions.
- *Data-snooping bias:* Using too many parameters to fit historical data, and avoiding it using large enough sample, out-of-sample testing, and sensitivity analysis.
- *Transaction cost:* Impact of transaction costs on performance.
- *Strategy refinement:* Common ways to make small variations on the strategy to optimize performance.

After going through this chapter and working through some of the examples and exercises, you should have gained some hands-on experience in how to retrieve historical data and backtest a strategy with either Excel or MATLAB.

When one starts testing a strategy, it may not be possible to avoid all these pitfalls due to constraints of time and other resources. In this case, it is okay to skip a few precautions to achieve a quick sense of whether the strategy has potential and is worthy of closer examination. Sometimes, even the most thorough and careful backtest cannot reveal problems that would be obvious after a few months of paper or real trading. One can always revisit each of these issues after the model has gone live.

Once you have backtested a strategy with reasonable performance, you are now ready to take the next step in setting up your trading business.

CHAPTER 4

Setting Up Your Business

In this chapter, we will be taking a break from the technical aspect of trading to focus on the business side of it. Assuming that your goal is to remain an independent trader and not work for a money management institution, the choice of the business structure for trading is important. The main choice you have to make is whether to open a retail brokerage account or to join a proprietary trading firm. The next step is to determine what features of the brokerage or trading firm are important to you. Finally, you have to decide what kind of physical trading infrastructure you need in order to execute your quantitative strategy.

BUSINESS STRUCTURE: RETAIL OR PROPRIETARY?

As a trader, you can choose to be completely independent or semi-independent. To be completely independent, you can simply open a retail brokerage account, deposit some cash, and start trading. No one will question your strategy, and no one will guide you in your trading. Furthermore, your leverage is limited by Securities and Exchange Commission (SEC) Regulation T—roughly two times your equity if you hold overnight positions. Naturally, all the profits and losses will accrue to you.

However, you can choose to join what is called a "proprietary trading firm" such as Bright Trading, ECHOtrade, or Genesis Securities, and become a member of their firm. In order to become a member of such firms, you have to pass the National Association of Securities Dealers (NASD) Series 7 examination to qualify you as a registered representative of a brokerage. You will still need to invest your own capital to start an account, but you will obtain much higher leverage (or "buying power") than is available through a retail account. Depending on how much capital you invested, you may get to keep all your profits, or some percentage of them. In terms of liability, however, your loss is limited to your initial investment. (Actually, liability is also limited if you form an S corporation or limited liability company [LLC] and open an account through this entity at a retail brokerage.) Often, you can also receive training from the firm, perhaps at an extra cost. You will also be subject to the various rules and regulations that the proprietary trading firm chooses to impose on its members, in addition to rules imposed by the SEC or NASD.

I made them sound like bad things when I spoke of rules and regulations imposed by proprietary trading firms. But, actually, some of these rules (such as the prohibition from trading penny stocks or the prohibition from carrying short positions overnight) are actually risk management measures for your own protection. Often, when the going is good, traders will bemoan these constraints limiting their flexibility and profitability. They may even decide to start their own retail trading accounts and start trading on their own. However, when they suffer the (almost inevitable) big drawdown, they wish that someone were there to restrain their risk appetites and come to regret this unfettered freedom. (The teenager in us has never left after all.)

The decision whether to go retail or to join a proprietary trading firm is generally based on your need of capital, the style of your strategy, and your skill level. For example, if you run a low-risk, market-neutral strategy that nevertheless requires a much higher leverage than allowed by Regulation T in order to generate good returns, a proprietary account may be better for you. However, if you engage in high-frequency futures trading that does not require too much capital, a retail account may save you a lot of costs and hassles. Similarly, a very experienced trader with strong risk management practices and emotional stability probably doesn't need the guidance given by a proprietary firm, but less experienced traders may benefit from the imposed restraints.

There is another consideration that applies to those of you who have discovered some unique, highly profitable strategies. In this situation, you may prefer to open a retail trading account, because if you trade through a proprietary account, your proprietary trading firm is going to find out about your highly profitable strategy and may "piggyback" on your strategy with a lot of its own capital. In this case, your strategy will suffer more market impact trading cost as time goes on.

Table 4.1 summarizes the pros and cons for each choice.

One final note: Some may think that there is a tax advantage in joining a proprietary trading firm because any trading loss can be deducted from current income instead of as capital loss. Actually, you can choose to apply for trader tax status even if you have a retail brokerage account so that your trading loss can offset other income, and not just other capital gain. For details on the tax considerations of a trading business, you can visit, for example, www.greencompany.com.

CHOOSING A BROKERAGE OR PROPRIETARY TRADING FIRM

Many traders use only one criterion to choose their brokerage or a proprietary trading firm to join: the commission rate. This is clearly an important criterion because if a trading strategy has a small return, high commissions may render it unprofitable. However, there are other important considerations.

Commissions actually form only part of your total transaction costs, sometimes even a small part. The speed of execution of your brokerage as well as their access of the so-called "dark-pool"

TABLE 4.1   Retail versus Proprietary Trading

Issue	Retail Trading	Proprietary Trading
Legal requirement to open account.	None.	Need to pass NASD Series 7 examination and satisfy other NASD-imposed restrictions.
Initial capital requirement.	Substantial.	Small.
Available leverage or buying power.	Determined by SEC Regulation T. Generally 2x leverage for overnight positions, and 4x for intraday positions.	Based on firm's discretion. Can be as high as 20x or more for intraday or hedged positions.
Liability to losses.	Unlimited, unless account is opened through an S corporation or LLC.	Limited to initial investment.
Commissions and fees.	Low commissions (perhaps less than 0.5 cent a share) and minimal monthly fees for data.	Higher commissions and significant monthly fees.
Bankruptcy risk of brokerage.	No risk. Account insured by Securities Investor Protection Corporation (SIPC).	Has risk. Account not insured.
Training, mentoring, guidance.	None.	May provide such services, sometimes at a fee.
Disclosure of trade secrets.	Little or no risk, especially if retail brokerage does not have proprietary trading unit.	Has risk. Managers can easily "piggyback" on profitable strategies.
Restrictions on trading style.	No restrictions, as long as it is allowed by SEC.	May have restrictions, such as prohibitions on holding overnight short positions.
Risk management.	Mostly self-imposed.	More comprehensive and imposed by managers.

liquidity also figures into your transaction costs. Dark-pool liquidity is formed by institutional orders facilitated away from the exchanges, or they come from the crossing of internal brokerage customer orders. These orders are not displayed as bid and ask quotes. Some of the "alternative trading systems" that provide dark-pool liquidity are Liquidnet and ITG's Posit. Your brokerage may use one or more of these providers, it may only use its internal crossing network, or it may use no alternative trading systems at all.

Sometimes, a better execution price at a large brokerage due to its state-of-the-art execution system and high-speed access to deeper dark pools of liquidity will more than compensate for its higher commissions. This kind of cost/benefit analysis cannot easily be carried out unless you actually trade on multiple brokerages simultaneously and compare the actual execution costs.

For example, I trade through Goldman Sachs's REDIPlus trading platform, whose Sigma X execution engine routes orders to both its internal crossing network as well as to external liquidity providers. I have found that it often improves my execution price by more than a few cents per share over execution on Interactive Brokers: more than enough to offset its higher commissions.

Another consideration is the range of products you can trade. Many retail brokerages or proprietary trading firms do not allow you to trade futures or foreign currencies. This would be a serious limitation to your trading business's growth.

Following these two fairly generic criteria, for a quantitative trader, the next important one is: Does the trading platform offer an application programming interface (API) so that your trading software can receive live data feed, generate orders, and automatically transmit the orders for execution in your account? I will discuss more about API in Chapter 5. The only point to note here is that without an API, high-frequency quantitative trading is impossible.

Closely related to the availability of API is the availability of paper trading accounts. If a brokerage does not offer you a paper trading account, it is very hard to test an API without risking real losses. Among the brokerages I know that offer paper trading accounts are Interactive Brokers, Genesis Securities, PFG Futures (for futures trading), and Oanda (for currency trading).

In addition to paper trading accounts, some brokerages provide a "simulator" account (an example is the demo account from Interactive Brokers), where quotes from the past are displayed as if they were real-time quotes, and an automated trading program can trade against these quotes at any time of the day in order to debug the program.

Finally, the reputation and financial strength of the proprietary trading firm you are considering is also important. This does not matter to the choice of a retail brokerage because, as noted in Table 4.1, retail accounts are insured by the SIPC whereas proprietary accounts are not. Hence, it is important that a proprietary trading firm has a strong balance sheet and good risk management practices to prevent the firm from collapsing because of bad trades made by its fellow member traders. (WorldCom's and Refco's collapses are good examples.) You should also make sure the firm is a broker-dealer registered with an exchange, so that it is regularly audited by the exchange and the SEC. (As of this writing, non-broker-dealer proprietary trading firms may all get shut down by the SEC anyway, starting with Tuco Trading in March 2008.) Furthermore, even if times are good for the firm, does it have a good reputation for easy redemption of your capital should you choose to do so? It is, of course, difficult for an outsider to assess whether a proprietary trading firm has such good attributes, but you can read about the firm's reputation based on their current or ex-members' opinions at the online forum www.elitetrader.com.

If you are undecided whether to open a retail brokerage account or a proprietary account, or which retail brokerage or proprietary firm to use, you can in fact do both, or open multiple accounts. Unlike finding full-time employment in proprietary trading firms, just joining them as a member, especially a remote-access member, does not usually compel you to sign a noncompete agreement. You are free to be a member of more than one proprietary firm, or have both proprietary and retail trading accounts, as long as this fact is fully disclosed to the proprietary trading firms involved and to the NASD as "outside business activities" and prior permissions obtained. With multiple accounts, it should be easier for you decide which cost structure is more beneficial to you and which account has the better infrastructure and tools for your automated trading system. And, in fact, sometimes each account has its own pros and cons, and you may want to have the flexibility of keeping all of them open for trading different strategies!

PHYSICAL INFRASTRUCTURE

Now that you have set up the legal and administrative structure of your trading business, it is time to consider the physical infrastructure. This applies to both retail and proprietary traders: Many proprietary trading firms allow their members to trade remotely in their homes. If you are a proprietary trader who requires minimal coaching from your account manager and are confident in your ability to set up the physical trading infrastructure yourself, there is no reason not to trade remotely.

In the start-up phase of your business, the physical infrastructure can be light and simple. You probably have all the components you need in your home office already: a good personal computer (practically any new computer with dual-core processors will do), a high-speed (DSL or cable) Internet connection, and, less well known, an uninterruptible power supply (UPS) so that your computer doesn't get accidentally shut down in the middle of a trade because of electricity fluctuations. The total initial investment should not exceed a couple of thousand dollars at the maximum, and the monthly cost should not be more than $50 or so if you don't already subscribe to cable TV.

Some traders wonder if having a TV tuned to CNBC or CNN is a good idea. While it certainly won't hurt, many professional quantitative traders have found that it is not necessary, as long as they also subscribe to another professional real-time newsfeed, such as Thomson Reuters, Dow Jones, or Bloomberg. While Bloomberg can cost almost $2,000 a month, various plans offered by Thomson Reuters and Dow Jones can cost as little as $100 to $200 (though some will require an annual contract). Bloomberg also has a free Internet radio stream at www.bloomberg.com/tvradio/radio that announces breaking business news and commentaries. Also, instead of installing a TV in your office, you can subscribe to CNBC Plus, which will provide live streaming video to your computer. Of course, too much real-time information may not necessarily lead to more profitable trades. For example, Michael Mauboussin of Legg Mason cites a study that finds horse-racing handicappers less successful in their predictions when they are given more information when ranking horses. (See *Economist*, 2007a, or Oldfield, 2007.)

As your trading business grows, you may upgrade your infrastructure gradually. Perhaps you will purchase faster computers. A quad-core computer at the time of this writing is considered fairly high end. Of course, when you are reading this, an octal-core or better personal computer will probably be widely available. According to a *New York Times* article (Markoff, 2007), PCs with octal-core chips will be available as soon as 2010.

You will certainly want to purchase multiple monitors to hook up to the same computer so that you have extended screen space to monitor all the different trading applications and portfolios. Maybe you will want to upgrade your Internet connection to a T1 line, too. As discussed in Chapter 2, any delay in the transmission of your order to your brokerage results in slippage, which is quite real in terms of lost profits. In fast-moving markets, every millisecond counts, and an upgrade in your Internet connection speed may well pay for itself very quickly. (A T1 line can cost anywhere from $700 to $1,500, whereas a cable/DSL connection is usually under $50. A T1 line transmits information at 1.5Mbps, where bps means "bits per second," about twice as fast as a cable/DSL connection.)

Once you have finally tested your trading strategy and discover that it works in practice very well, it will be time to scale up the business and consider "business continuity planning" so that your trading strategy is resilient to common household disasters such as Internet outage, electricity outage, flooding, and so on. You can install your trading programs on a remote server located in a hosting company; in fact, you can even "collocate" your computers containing your trading programs at the hosting company. (Having your programs hosted or having your servers collocated will cost you anywhere from hundreds to over a thousand dollars a month.) You can monitor, maintain, or update your trading programs running on these servers remotely through common remote PC applications such as GotoMyPC (about $15 a month), while the remote servers will be sending orders directly to your brokerage. The advantage of this setup is not only that your trading will almost never have downtime, but that the Internet connection at the hosting company is likely to be faster than what you have at home or in your office. In fact, for some ultra-high-frequency trading applications, it is advantageous to locate your servers near an Internet backbone as close as possible to the exchange on which your trades will be executed. Just Google the phrases "server hosting" or "collocation servers" and you will find numerous hosting firms offering such services.

SUMMARY

This chapter focused on those decisions and steps that you need to take to bridge the research phase and the execution phase of your trading business. I have covered the pros and cons of retail trading versus proprietary trading and the issues to consider in choosing a brokerage or proprietary trading firm.

In a nutshell, retail brokerages give you complete freedom and better capital protection but smaller leverage, while proprietary trading firms give you less freedom and less capital protection but much high leverage. Finding a suitable retail brokerage is relatively easy. It took me less than a month to research and settle on one and I have not found a reason to switch yet. Finding a suitable proprietary trading firm is much more involved, since there are contracts to sign and an exam (Series 7) to pass. It took me several months to get my account set up at one.

Of course, you can choose to have both retail and proprietary accounts, each tailored to the specific needs of your strategies. This way, you can also easily compare their speed of execution and depth of liquidity.

Regardless of whether you have chosen to trade in a retail brokerage or join a proprietary trading firm, you need to make sure their trading account and systems have these features:

- Relatively low commissions.
- Trade a good variety of financial instruments.
- Access to deep pool of liquidity.
- Most importantly, API for real-time data retrieval and order transmission.

I also described the progressive buildup of the physical infrastructure you need to build in order to run a trading business. Some of the components of a trader's operating environment mentioned are:

- A dual-core or quad-core computer.
- A high-speed Internet connection (cable, DSL, or T1).
- A noninterruptible power supply.
- Real-time data and news feed and subscription to financial TV news channels.
- Server hosting or collocation.

Building out the physical trading infrastructure is actually quite easy, since in the beginning you probably have all the components ready in your home office already. I have found that it is easy to trade a million-dollar portfolio with nothing more than a few thousand dollars' initial investment in your physical infrastructure, and a few hundred dollars a month in operating cost. But if you want to increase your trading capacity or improve your returns, additional incremental investments will be needed.

Once you have considered and taken these steps, you are now positioned to build an automated trading environment to execute your strategy, which will be covered in the next chapter.

CHAPTER 5

Execution Systems

A t this point, you should have backtested a good strategy (maybe something like the pair-trading strategy in Example 3.6), picked a brokerage (e.g., Interactive Brokers), and have set up a good operating environment (at first, nothing more than a computer, a high-speed Internet connection, and a real-time news-feed). You are almost ready to execute your trading strategy—after you have implemented an automated trading system (ATS) to generate and transmit your orders to your brokerage for execution. This chapter is about building such an automated trading system and ways to minimize trading costs and divergence with your expected performance based on your backtests.

WHAT AN AUTOMATED TRADING SYSTEM CAN DO FOR YOU

An automated trading system will retrieve up-to-date market data from your brokerage or other data vendors, run a trading algorithm to generate orders, and submit those orders to your brokerage for execution. Sometimes, all these steps are fully automated and implemented as one desktop application installed on your computer. Other times, only part of this process is automated, and you would have to take some manual steps to complete the whole procedure.

A fully automated system has the advantage that it minimizes human errors and delays. For certain high-frequency systems, a fully automated system is indispensable, because any human intervention will cause enough delay to seriously derail the performance. However, a fully automated system is also complicated and costly to build, often requiring professional programmers with knowledge of high-performance programming languages such as Java, C#, or C++ in order to connect to your brokerage's application programming interface (API).

For lower-frequency quantitative trading strategies, there is a semiautomated alternative: One can generate the orders using programs such as Excel or MATLAB, then submit those orders using built-in tools such as a basket trader or spread trader offered by your brokerage. If your brokerage provides a dynamic data exchange (DDE) link to Excel (see below), you can also write a macro attached to your Excel spreadsheet that allows you to submit orders to the brokerage simply by running the macro. This way, there is no need to build an application in a complicated programming language. However, it does mean that you would have to perform quite a few manual steps in order to submit your orders.

Whether you have built a semiautomated or a fully automated trading system, there is often a need for input data beyond the prices that your brokerage or data vendor can readily provide you. For example, earnings estimates or dividends data are often not provided as part of the real-time data stream. These nonprice data are typically available free of charge from many web sites, but are usually embedded in an HTML format and not readily usable. Hence, an automated system also must be able to retrieve such web pages, parse them, and reformat them into a tabular format that your trading strategy can utilize. Such web page retrieval and parsing programs can readily be implemented in MATLAB (see Example 3.1 in Chapter 3), or in other scripting languages such as Perl.

I will discuss some details of the two kinds of system in the following sections. I will also discuss how to hire a programming consultant in case you would like someone to help automate the execution of your trading strategy.

Building a Semiautomated Trading System

In a semiautomated trading system (shown in Figure 5.1), a user typically generates a list of orders using familiar and easy-to-use software such as Excel or MATLAB. Often, the program that generates this order list is the same as the backtest program: After all, you are implementing the same quantitative strategy that you have backtested. Of course, you must remember to update the input data file to reflect the most recent data. This is usually done with either a MATLAB program that can directly go to a web site to retrieve the appropriate data, or with a separate program such as HQuote, mentioned earlier, which can download en masse historical price data for a large number of symbols. In the latter case, MATLAB is used only to organize those data in a suitable format for the trading strategy program that generates today's orders.

The data update step is easy when the most recent data is the previous day's close, but certainly more difficult when it is the last intraday price. When the data required is the last price, your data vendor or brokerage must provide a DDE link that automatically

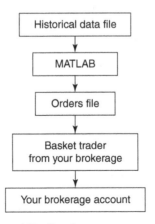

FIGURE 5.1 Semiautomated Trading System

updates an Excel input file. Most brokerages that cater to serious traders provide such DDE links. Interactive Brokers, Genesis Securities, and Goldman Sachs's REDIPlus are some of the examples. Many proprietary trading firms use one of these brokerages for execution; hence, you would have access to the full menu of these brokerages' real-time data and order entry technologies as well.

A DDE link is just an expression to be inserted on an Excel spreadsheet that will automatically load the appropriate data into a cell. The expression is different for different brokerages, but they generally look like this:

```
=accountid|LAST!IBM
```

where LAST indicates the last price is requested, and IBM is the symbol in question.

To generate the orders, you can run an Excel macro (a Visual Basic program attached to the spreadsheet) or a MATLAB program, which scans through the information and prices on the spreadsheet, runs the trading algorithm, and writes out the orders to another text file where each line contains the triplet (symbol, side, size). For example,

```
("IBM", "BUY", "100")
```

may be a line in the output order file. Sometimes, your brokerage requires other information for order submission, such as whether the order is Day only, or Good Till Cancel. All this auxiliary information is written out to each line of the order file.

After the text file containing the order list is generated, you can then upload this order file to your brokerage's basket trader or spread trader for submission.

A basket trader is an application that allows you to upload multiple orders for multiple symbols and submit them to the brokerage in one keystroke. Spread trader is an application with which you can specify the symbols of multiple pairs of stocks or other securities, and the conditions when orders for each of these pairs should be entered. The spread trader can monitor real-time prices and check whether these conditions are satisfied throughout the trading day.

If the DDE links of your brokerage allow you to submit orders, you can also run an Excel macro to sweep through the order file and submit all the orders to your account with one press of the button as well.

The two brokerages that I use, Interactive Brokers and REDIPlus, have basket trader and spread trader, as well as DDE links for data update and order submission as part of their execution platform. (Interactive Brokers' spread trader can be used only for futures calendar spreads. Stock spreads can be specified one pair at a time through their so-called "Generic Combo," though the continuous monitoring of order entry condition works for both futures and stocks.)

Here is what I do with a basket trader from Interactive Brokers. Every day before the market opens I run a MATLAB program that retrieves market data, run the trading algorithm, and write out a list of orders into an order file that can be over 1,000 lines (corresponding to over 1,000 symbols). I then bring up the basket trader from my trading screen, upload the order file to my account using the basket trader, and in one keystroke submit them all to my account. Some of these orders may get executed at the open; others may get executed later or not at all. Before the market closes, I cancel all the unexecuted orders by pressing a button. Finally, if I want to exit all the existing positions, I simply press another button in the basket trader to generate the appropriate exit orders.

I use REDIPlus's spread trader for pair-trading strategies such as Example 3.6 because I can have the spread trader enter orders at all times of the day, not just at the market close. Again, before the market opens I use MATLAB to retrieve market data, run the pair-trading algorithm, and write out limit prices for all the pairs in my universe. (Note that the limit prices are limits on the spread, not on the individual stocks. If they were on the individual stocks, ordinary limit orders would have done the trick and the spread trader would have been redundant.) I then go to the spread trader, which already contains all these pairs that I have previously specified, and manually adjust the limit prices based on the MATLAB output. (Actually, this step can be automated too—all the spread orders information can be written out to an Excel file by MATLAB and uploaded to the spread trader.) Pressing another button will initiate automatic monitoring of prices and entering of orders throughout the trading day.

I also use RediPlus's DDE link for submitting orders for another basket trading strategy. I use MATLAB to generate the appropriate DDE link formula in each Excel cell so that it can automatically update the appropriate data for the particular symbol on that row. After the market opens, I run a macro attached to that spreadsheet, which scans through each symbol and submits it (together with other order information contained in the spreadsheet) to my account at REDIPlus.

Typically, a semiautomated trading system is suitable if you need to run this step only a few times a day in order to generate one or a few waves of orders. Even if your brokerage's API provides an order submission function for your use in an Excel Visual Basic macro, its speed is usually too slow if you have to run this program frequently in order to capture the latest data and generate wave after wave of orders. In this case, one must build a fully automated trading system.

Building a Fully Automated Trading System

A fully automated trading system (see Figure 5.2) can run the trading algorithm in a loop again and again, constantly scanning the latest prices and generating new waves of orders throughout the trading day. The submission of orders through an API to your brokerage account is automatic, so you would not need to load the trades to a basket trader or spread trader, or even manually run a macro on

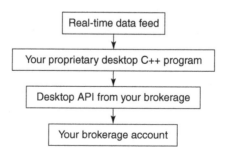

FIGURE 5.2 Fully Automated Trading System

your Excel spreadsheet. All you need to do is press a "start" button in the morning, and then a "close" button at the end of the day, and your program will do all the trading for you.

Implementing a fully automated system requires that your brokerage provides an API for data retrieval and order submission. Your brokerage will usually provide API for some popular programming languages such as Visual Basic, Java, C#, or C++, so your fully automated system must also be written in one of these languages. Unfortunately, no brokerage that I know of provides an API for MATLAB. Hence, MATLAB cannot be used to build the order transmission portion of an automated trading system.

Theoretically, a fully automated system can be constructed out of an Excel spreadsheet and an attached macro: All you have to do is to create a loop in your macro so that it updates the cells using the DDE links and submit orders when appropriate continuously throughout the day. Unfortunately, data updates through DDE links are slow, and generally your brokerage limits the number of symbols that you can update all at once. (Unless you have generated a large amount of commissions in the previous trading month, Interactive Brokers allows you to update only 100 symbols by default.) Similarly, order submissions through DDE links are also slow. Hence, for trading strategies that react to real-time market data changes intraday, this setup using a spreadsheet is not feasible.

There are some brokerages such as TradeStation that offer a complete backtesting and order submission platform. If you backtested on such a platform, then it is trivial to configure it so that the program will submit real orders to your account. This dispenses with the need to write your own software, whether for backtesting or for automated execution. However, as I mentioned in Chapter 3, the drawback of such proprietary systems is that they are seldom as flexible as a general-purpose programming language like MATLAB or Java for the construction of your strategy. For instance, if you want to pursue a rather mathematically complex strategy based on principal component analysis (such as the one in Example 7.4), it would be quite difficult to backtest in TradeStation. More advanced integrated trading platforms such as Alphacet's Discovery do provide a much larger variety of algorithms to be backtested and implemented, but they may not be affordable to the typical independent trader.

HIRING A PROGRAMMING CONSULTANT

Building an ATS generally requires more professional programming skills than backtesting a strategy. This is especially true for high-frequency strategies where the speed of execution is of the essence. Instead of implementing an execution system yourself, you may find that hiring a programming consultant will result in much less headache.

Hiring a programming consultant does not have to be expensive. For an experienced programmer, the hourly fees may range from $50 to $100. Sometimes, you can negotiate a fixed fee for the entire project ahead of time, and I find that most projects for independent traders can be done with $1,000 to $5,000. If you have an account at one of the brokerages that supply you with an API, the brokerage can often refer you to some programmers who have experience with their API. (Interactive Brokers, for example, has a special web page that allows programming consultants to offer their services.) You can also look around (or post a request) on elitetrader.com for such programmers. As a last resort, you can find hundreds if not thousands of freelance programmers advertising themselves on craigslist.org. However, I find that the quality of freelance programmers on craigslist can be uneven—in particular, they usually lack in-depth knowledge of financial markets and trading technology, which can be crucial to successfully implementing an automated trading system.

There is one issue that may worry you as you consider hiring programmers: How do you keep your trading strategy confidential? Of course, you can have them sign nondisclosure agreements (NDAs, downloadable for free at many legal document web sites), but it is almost impossible to find out if the programmers are in fact running your strategies in their personal accounts once the programs are implemented. There are several ways to address this concern.

First, as I mentioned before, most strategies that you may think are your unique creations are actually quite well known to experienced traders. So, whether you like it or not, other people are already trading very similar strategies and impacting your returns. Adding an extra trader or two, unless the trader works for an institutional money manager, is not likely to cause much more impact.

Second, if you are trading a strategy that has a large capacity (e.g., most futures trading strategies), then the extra market impact from your rogue programmer consultant will be minimal.

Finally, you can choose to compartmentalize your information and implementation—that is, you can hire different programmers to build different parts of the automated trading strategy. Often, one programmer can build an automated trading infrastructure program that can be used for different strategies, and another one can implement the actual strategy, which will read in input parameters. So in this case, the first programmer does not know your strategy, and the second programmer does not have the infrastructure to execute the strategy. Furthermore, neither programmer knows the actual parameter values to use for your strategy.

MINIMIZING TRANSACTION COSTS

We saw in Chapter 3 how transaction costs can impact a strategy's actual return. Besides changing your brokerage or proprietary trading firm to one that charges a lower commission, there are a few things you can do in your execution method to minimize the transaction costs.

To cut down on commissions, you can refrain from trading low-price stocks. Typically, institutional traders do not trade any stocks with prices lower than $5. Not only do low-price stocks increase your total commissions costs (since you need to buy or sell more shares for a fixed amount of capital), percentage-wise they also have a wider bid-ask spread and therefore increase your total liquidity costs.

In order to minimize market impact cost, you should limit the size (number of shares) of your orders based on the liquidity of the stock. One common measure of liquidity is the average daily volume (it is your choice what lookback period you want to average over). As a rule of thumb, each order should not exceed 1 percent of the average daily volume. As an independent trader, you may think that it is not easy to reach this 1 percent threshold, and you would be right when the stock in question is a large-cap stock belonging to the S&P 500. However, you may be surprised by the low liquidity of some small-cap stocks out there.

For example, at the time of this writing, IRN is a stock in the S&P 600 SmallCap Index. It has a three-month average volume of about 51,000, and it closed today at $4.45. So 1 percent of this average volume is just 510 shares, which are worth only $2,269!

Another way to reduce market impact is to scale the size of your orders based on the market capitalization of a stock. The way to scale the size is not an exact science, but most practitioners would not recommend a linear scale because the market capitalization of companies varies over several orders of magnitude, from tens of millions to hundreds of billions. A linear scale (i.e., scaling the capital of a stock to be linearly proportional to its market capitalization) would result in practically zero weights for most small- and micro-cap stocks in your portfolio, and this will take away any benefits of diversification. If we were to use linear scale, the capital weight of the largest large-cap stock will be about 10,000 of the smallest small-cap stock. To reap the benefits of diversification, we should not allow that ratio to be more than 10 or so, provided that the liquidity (volume) constraint described above is also satisfied. If the capital weight of a stock is proportional to the fourth root of its market cap, it would do the trick.

There is one other way to reduce market impact. Many institutional traders who desire to execute a large order will break it down into many smaller orders and execute them over time. This method of trading will certainly reduce market impact; however, it engenders another kind of transactions costs, namely, slippage. As discussed in Chapter 2, slippage is the difference between the price that triggers the trading signal and the average execution price of the entire order. Because the order is executed over a period of time, slippage can be quite large. Since reducing market impact in this way may increase slippage, it is not really suitable for retail traders whose order size is usually not big enough to require this remedy.

Sometimes, however, slippage is outside of your control: Perhaps your brokerage's execution speed is simply too slow, due to either software issues (their software processes your orders too slowly), risk control issues (your order has to be checked against your account's buying power and pass various risk control criteria before it can be routed to the exchange), or pipeline issues (the brokerage's speed of access to the exchanges). Or perhaps your brokerage does not have access to deep enough "dark-pool" liquidity. These execution costs and issues should affect your choice of brokerages, as I pointed out in Chapter 4.

TESTING YOUR SYSTEM BY PAPER TRADING

After you have built your automated trading system, it is a good idea to test it in a paper trading account, if your brokerage provides one. Paper trading has a number of benefits; chief among them is that this is practically the only way to see if your ATS software has bugs without losing a lot of real money.

Often, the moment you start paper trading you will realize that there is a glaring look-ahead bias in your strategy—there may just be no way you could have obtained some crucial piece of data before you enter an order! If this happens, it is "back to the drawing board."

You should be able run your ATS, execute paper trades, and then compare the paper trades and profit and loss (P&L) with the theoretical ones generated by your backtest program using the latest data. If the difference is not due to transaction costs (including an expected delay in execution for the paper trades), then your software likely has bugs. (I mentioned the names of some of the brokerages that offer paper trading accounts in Chapter 4.)

Another benefit of paper trading is that it gives you better intuitive understanding of your strategy, including the volatility of its P&L, the typical amount of capital utilized, the number of trades per day, and the various operational difficulties including data issues. Even though you can theoretically check out most of these features of your strategy in a backtest, one will usually gain intuition only if one faces them on a daily, ongoing basis. Backtesting also won't reveal the operational difficulties, such as how fast you can download all the needed data before the market opens each day and how you can optimize your operational procedures in actual execution.

(Do not underestimate the time required for preparing your orders before the market opens. It took me some 20 minutes to download and parse all my historical data each morning, and it took another 15 minutes or so to transmit all the orders to my account. If your trading strategy depends on data or news prior to the market open that cannot be more than 35 minutes old, then you need to either figure out a different execution environment or modify your strategy. It is hard to figure out all these timing issues until paper trading is conducted.)

If you are able to run a paper trading system for a month or longer, you may even be able to discover data-snooping bias, since paper trading is a true out-of-sample test. However, traders usually pay less and less attention to the performance of a paper trading system as time goes on, since there are always more pressing issues (such as the real trading programs that are being run). This inattention causes the paper trading system to perform poorly because of neglect and errors in operation. So data-snooping bias can usually be discovered only when you have actually started trading the system with a small amount of capital.

WHY DOES ACTUAL PERFORMANCE DIVERGE FROM EXPECTATIONS?

Finally, after much hard work testing and preparing, you have entered your first order and it got executed! Whether you win or lose, you understand that it will take a while to find out if its performance meets your expectations. But what if after one month, then two months, and then finally a quarter has passed, the strategy still delivers a meager or maybe even negative returns. This disappointing experience is common to freshly minted quantitative traders. This would be the time to review the list of what possibly may have caused this divergence from expectation. Start with the simplest diagnosis:

- Do you have bugs in your ATS software?
- Do the trades generated by your ATS match the ones generated by your backtest program?
- Are the execution costs much higher than what you expected?
- Are you trading illiquid stocks that caused a lot of market impact?

If the execution costs are much higher than what you expected, it may be worthwhile to reread the section on how to minimize transaction costs again.

After these easy diagnoses have been eliminated, one is then faced with the two most dreaded causes of divergence: data-snooping bias and regime shifts.

To see if data-snooping bias is causing the underperformance of your live trading, try to eliminate as many rules and as many parameters in your strategy as possible. If the backtest performance completely fell apart after this exercise, chances are you do have this bias and it is time to look for a new strategy. If the backtest performance is still reasonable, your poor live trading performance may just be due to bad luck.

Regime shifts refer to the situation when the financial market structure or the macroeconomic environment undergoes a drastic change so much so that trading strategies that were profitable before may not be profitable now.

There are two noteworthy regime shifts in recent years related to market (or regulatory) structure that may affect certain strategies.

The first one is the decimalization of stock prices. Prior to early 2001, stock prices in the United States were quoted in multiples of one-sixteenth and one-eighteenth of a penny. Since April 9, 2001, all U.S. stocks have been quoted in decimals. This seemingly innocuous change has had a dramatic impact on the market structure, which is particularly negative for the profitability of statistical arbitrage strategies.

The reason for this may be worthy of a book unto itself. In a nutshell, decimalization reduces frictions in the price discovery process, while statistical arbitrageurs mostly act as market makers and derive their profits from frictions and inefficiencies in this process. (This is the explanation given by Dr. Andrew Sterge in a Columbia University financial engineering seminar titled "Where Have All the Stat Arb Profits Gone?" in January 2008. Other industry practitioners have made the same point to me in private conversations.) Hence, we can expect backtest performance of statistical arbitrage strategies prior to 2001 to be far superior to their present-day performance.

The other regime shift is relevant if your strategy shorts stocks.

Prior to 2007, Securities and Exchange Commission (SEC) rules state that one cannot short a stock unless it is on a "plus tick" or "zero-plus tick." Hence, if your backtest data include those earlier days, it is possible that a very profitable short position could not actually have been entered into due to a lack of plus ticks, or it could have been entered into only with a large slippage. This plus-tick rule was eliminated by the SEC in June 2007. Therefore, your backtest results for a strategy that shorts stocks may show an artificially inflated performance prior to 2007 relative to their actual realizable performance in those days.

Actually, there is another problem with realizing the backtest performance of a strategy that shorts stocks apart from this regulatory regime shift. Even without the plus-tick rule, many stocks, especially the small-cap ones or the ones with low liquidity, are "hard to borrow." For you to be able to short a stock, your broker has to be able to borrow it from someone else (usually a large mutual fund or other brokerage clients) and lend it to you for selling. If no one is able or willing to lend you their stock, it is deemed hard to borrow and you would not be able to short it. Hence, again, a very profitable historical short position may not actually have been possible due to the difficulty of borrowing the stock.

The two regime shifts described here are the obvious and well-publicized ones. However, there may be other, more subtle regime shifts that apply to your category of stocks that few people know about, but is no less disruptive to the profitability of your strategy's performance. I will discuss how one might come up with a model that detects regime shifts automatically as one of the special topics of Chapter 7.

SUMMARY

An automated trading system is a piece of software that automatically generates and transmits orders to your brokerage account based on your trading strategy. The advantages of having this software are that:

- It ensures the faithful adherence to your backtested strategy.
- It eliminates manual operation so that you can simultaneously run multiple strategies.
- Most importantly, it allows speedy transmissions of orders, which is essential to high-frequency trading strategies.

Regarding the difference between a semiautomated trading system and a fully automated trading system:

- In a semiautomated trading system, the trader still needs to manually upload a text file containing order details to a basket trader or spread trader, and manually press a button to transmit the orders at the appropriate time. However, the order text file can be automatically generated by a program such as MATLAB.
- In a fully automated trading system, the program will be able to automatically upload data and transmit orders throughout the trading day or even over many days.

After the creation of an ATS, you can then focus on the various issues that are important in execution: minimizing transaction costs and paper trading. Minimizing transaction costs is mainly a matter of not allowing your order size to be too big relative to its average trading volume and relative to its market capitalization. Paper trading allows you to:

- Discover software bugs in your trading strategy and execution programs.
- Discover look-ahead or even data-snooping bias.
- Discover operating difficulties and plan for operating schedules.
- Estimate transaction costs more realistically.
- Gain important intuition about P&L volatility, capital usage, portfolio size, and trade frequency.

Finally, what do you do in the situation where your live trading underperforms your backtest? You can start by addressing the usual problems: Eliminate bugs in the strategy or execution software; reduce transaction costs; and simplify the strategy by eliminating parameters. But, fundamentally, your strategy still may have suffered from data-snooping bias or regime shift.

If you believe (and you can only believe, as you can never *prove* this) that your poor live trading performance is due to bad luck and not to data-snooping bias in your backtest nor to a regime shift, how should you proceed when the competing demands of perseverance and capital preservation seem to suggest opposite actions? This critical issue will be addressed in the next chapter, which discusses systematic ways to preserve capital in the face of losses and yet still be in a position to recover once the tide turns.

CHAPTER 6

Money and Risk Management

All trading strategies suffer occasional losses, technically known as drawdowns. The drawdowns may last a few minutes or a few years. To profit from a quantitative trading business, it is essential to manage your risks in a way that limits your drawdowns to a tolerable level and yet be positioned to use optimal leverage of your equity to achieve maximum possible growth of your wealth. Furthermore, if you have more than one strategy, you will also need to find a way to optimally allocate capital among them so as to maximize overall risk-adjusted return.

The optimal allocation of capital and the optimal leverage to use so as to strike the right balance between risk management and maximum growth is the focus of this chapter, and the central tool we use is called the Kelly formula.

OPTIMAL CAPITAL ALLOCATION AND LEVERAGE

Suppose you plan to trade several strategies, each with their own expected returns and standard deviations. How should you allocate capital among them in an optimal way? Furthermore, what should be the overall leverage (ratio of the size of your portfolio to your account equity)? Dr. Edward Thorp, whom I mentioned in the preface, has written an excellent expository article on this subject in one of his papers (Thorp, 1997), and I shall follow his discussion closely in this chapter. (Dr. Thorp's discussion is centered on a portfolio of securities, and mine is constructed around a portfolio of strategies. However, the mathematics are almost identical.)

Every optimization problem begins with an objective. Our objective here is to maximize our long-term wealth—an objective that I believe is not controversial for the individual investor. Maximizing long-term wealth is equivalent to maximizing the long-term compounded growth rate g of your portfolio. Note that this objective implicitly means that ruin (i.e., equity's going to zero or less because of a loss) must be avoided. This is because if ruin can be reached with nonzero probability at some point, the long-term wealth is surely zero, as is the long-term growth rate.

(In all of the discussions, I assume that we reinvest all trading profits, and therefore it is the levered, compounded growth rate that is of ultimate importance.)

One approximation that I will make is that the probability distribution of the returns of each of the trading strategy i is Gaussian, with a fixed mean m_i and standard deviation s_i. (The returns should be net of all financing costs; that is, they should be excess returns.) This is a common approximation in finance, but it can be quite inaccurate. Certain big losses in the financial markets occur with far higher frequencies (or viewed alternatively, at far higher magnitudes) than Gaussian probability distributions will allow. However, every scientific or engineering endeavor starts with the simplest model with the crudest approximation, and finance is no exception. I will discuss the remedies to such inaccuracies later in this chapter.

Let's denote the optimal fractions of your equity that you should allocate to each of your n strategies by a column vector $F^* = (f_1^*, f_2^*, \ldots, f_n^*)^{\mathrm{T}}$. Here, T means transpose.

Given our optimization objective and the Gaussian assumption, Dr. Thorp has shown that the optimal allocation is given by

$$F^* = C^{-1}M$$

Here, C is the covariance matrix such that matrix element C_{ij} is the covariance of the returns of the ith and j^{th} strategies, -1 indicates matrix inverse, and $M = (m_1, m_2, \ldots, m_n)^T$ is the column vector of mean returns of the strategies. Note that these returns are one-period, simple (uncompounded), unlevered returns. For example, if the strategy is long \$1 of stock A and short \$1 of stock B and made \$0.10 profit in a period, m is 0.05, no matter what the equity in the account is.

If we assume that the strategies are all statistically independent, the covariance matrix becomes a diagonal matrix, with the diagonal elements equal to the variance of the individual strategies. This leads to an especially simple formula:

$$f_i = m_i/s_i^2$$

This is the famous Kelly formula (for the many interesting stories surrounding this formula, see, for example, Poundstone, 2005) as applied to continuous finance as opposed to gambling with discrete outcomes, and it gives the optimal leverage one should employ for a particular trading strategy.

Interested readers can look up a simple derivation of Kelly formula at the end of this chapter in the simple one-strategy case.

Example 6.1: An Interesting Puzzle (or Why Risk Is Bad for You)*

Here is a little puzzle that may stymie many a professional trader. Suppose a certain stock exhibits a true (geometric) random walk, by which I mean there is a 50–50 chance that the stock is going up 1 percent or down 1 percent every minute. If you buy this stock, are you most likely—in the long run and ignoring financing costs—to make money, lose money, or be flat?

Most traders will blurt out the answer "Flat!," and that is wrong. The correct answer is that you will lose money, at the rate of 0.005 percent (or 0.5 basis point) every minute! This is because for a geometric random walk, the average compounded rate of return is not the short-term (or one-period) return m (0 here), but is $g = m - s^2/2$. This follows from the general formula for compounded growth $g(f)$ given in the appendix to this chapter, with the leverage f set to 1 and risk-free rate r set to 0. This is also consistent with the fact that the geometric mean of a set of numbers is always smaller than the arithmetic mean (unless the numbers are identical, in which case the two means are the same). When we assume, as I did, that the arithmetic mean of the returns is zero, the geometric mean, which gives the average compounded rate of return, must be negative.

The take-away lesson here is that risk always decreases long-term growth rate—hence the importance of risk management!

*This example was reproduced with corrections from my blog article "Maximizing Compounded Rate of Return," which you can find at epchan.blogspot.com/2006/10/maximizing-compounded-rate-of-return.html.

Often, because of uncertainties in parameter estimations, and also because return distributions are not really Gaussian, traders prefer to cut this recommended leverage in half for safety. This is called "half-Kelly" betting.

If you have a retail trading account, your maximum overall leverage l will be restricted to either 2 or 4, depending on whether you hold the positions overnight or just intraday. In this situation, you would have to reduce each f_i by the same factor $l/(|f_1| + |f_2| + \cdots + |f_n|)$, where $|f_1| + |f_2| + \cdots + |f_n|$ is the total unrestricted leverage of the portfolio. Here, we ignore the possibility that some of your individual strategies may hold positions that offset each other (such as a long and a short position each balanced with short and long T-bills, respectively) which may allow you to hold a higher leverage than this formula suggests.

I stated that adopting this capital allocation and leverage will allow us to maximize the long-term compounded growth rate of your equity. So what is this maximum compounded growth rate? It turns out to be

$$g = r + S^2/2$$

where the S is none other than the Sharpe ratio of your portfolio! As I mentioned in Chapter 2, the higher the Sharpe ratio of your portfolio (or strategy), the higher the maximum growth rate of your equity (or wealth), *provided* you use the optimal leverage recommended by the Kelly formula. Here is the simple mathematical embodiment of this fact.

Example 6.2: Calculating the Optimal Leverage Based on the Kelly Formula

Let's see an example of the Kelly formula at work. Suppose our portfolio consists of just a long position in SPY, the exchange-traded fund (ETF) tracking the S&P 500 index. Let's suppose that the mean annual return of SPY is 11.23 percent, with an annualized standard deviation of 16.91 percent, and that the risk-free rate is 4 percent. Hence, the portfolio has an annual mean excess return of 7.231 percent and an annual standard deviation of 16.91 percent, giving it a Sharpe ratio of 0.4275. The optimal leverage according to the Kelly formula is $f = 0.07231/0.1691^2 = 2.528$. (Notice one interesting tidbit: The Kelly f is independent of time scale, so it actually does not matter whether you annualize your return and standard deviation, as opposed to Sharpe ratio which is time scale dependent.) Finally, the annualized compounded, levered growth rate is 13.14 percent, which includes the financing costs.

You can verify these numbers yourselves by downloading the SPY daily prices from Yahoo! Finance and computing the various quantities on a spreadsheet. I did that on December 29, 2007, and my spreadsheet is available at epchan.com/book/example6_2.xls. In column H, I have computed the daily returns of the (adjusted) closing prices of SPY, while in row 3760 starting at column H, I have computed the (annualized) mean return of SPY, the standard deviation of SPY, the mean excess return of the portfolio, the Sharpe ratio of the portfolio, the Kelly leverage, and, finally, the compounded growth rate.

The Kelly leverage of 2.528 that we computed is saying that, for this strategy, if you have $100,000 in cash to invest, and if you really believe the expected values of your returns and standard deviations, you should borrow money to buy $252,800 worth of SPY. Furthermore, expect an annual compounded return on your $100,000 investment to be 13.14 percent.

For comparison, let's see what compounded growth rate we will get if we did not leverage our investment (see the formula in the appendix to this chapter): $g = r + m - s^2/2 = 0.1123 - (0.1691)^2/2 = 9.8$ percent. This, and not mean annual return of 11.23 percent, is the long-term growth rate of buying SPY with cash only.

Example 6.3: Calculating the Optimal Allocation Using Kelly Formula

We pick three sector-specific ETFs and see how we should allocate capital among them to achieve the maximum growth rate for the portfolio. The three ETFs are: OIH (oil service), RKH (regional bank), and RTH (retail). The daily prices are downloaded from Yahoo! Finance and saved in epchan.com/book as OIH.xls, RKH.xls, and RTH.xls. Here is the MATLAB program (epchan.com/book/example6_3.m) to retrieve these files and calculate *M*, *C*, and *F**.

```
% make sure previously defined variables are erased.
clear;
% read a spreadsheet named "OIH.xls" into MATLAB.
[num1, txt1]=xlsread('OIH');
% the first column (starting from the second row) is
% the trading days in format mm/dd/yyyy.
tday1=txt1(2:end, 1);
tday1=datestr(datenum(tday1, 'mm/dd/yyyy'), 'yyyym-
mdd'); % convert the format into yyyymmdd.

% convert the date strings first into cell arrays
% and then into numeric format.
tday1=str2double(cellstr(tday1));
% the last column contains the adjusted close prices.
adjcls1=num1(:, end);
% read a spreadsheet named "RKH.xls" into MATLAB.
[num2, txt2]=xlsread('RKH');
% the first column (starting from the second row) is
% the trading days in format mm/dd/yyyy.
tday2=txt2(2:end, 1);
% convert the format into yyyymmdd.
tday2=..
datestr(datenum(tday2, 'mm/dd/yyyy'), 'yyyymmdd');

% convert the date strings first into cell arrays and
% then into numeric format.
tday2=str2double(cellstr(tday2));
adjcls2=num2(:, end);

% read a spreadsheet named "RTH.xls" into MATLAB.
[num3, txt3]=xlsread('RTH');
% the first column (starting from the second row) is
% the trading days in format mm/dd/yyyy.
tday3=txt3(2:end, 1);
```

```
% convert the format into yyyymmdd.
tday3=..
datestr(datenum(tday3, 'mm/dd/yyyy'), 'yyyymmdd');

% convert the date strings first into cell arrays and
% then into numeric format.
tday3=str2double(cellstr(tday3));
adjcls3=num3(:, end);

% merge these data
tday=union(tday1, tday2);
tday=union(tday, tday3);
adjcls=NaN(length(tday), 3);

[foo idx1 idx]=intersect(tday1, tday);
adjcls(idx, 1)=adjcls1(idx1);
[foo idx2 idx]=intersect(tday2, tday);
adjcls(idx, 2)=adjcls2(idx2);
[foo idx3 idx]=intersect(tday3, tday);
adjcls(idx, 3)=adjcls3(idx3);

ret=(adjcls-lag1(adjcls))./lag1(adjcls); % returns

% days where any one return is missing
baddata=find(any(~isfinite(ret), 2));
% eliminate days where any one return is missing
ret(baddata,:)=[];
% excess returns: assume annualized risk free rate is 4%
excessRet=ret-repmat(0.04/252, size(ret));

% annualized mean excess returns
M=252*mean(excessRet, 1)'% M =
%
%      0.1396
%    0.0294
%   -0.0073

C=252*cov(excessRet) % annualized covariance matrix
% C =
%
%      0.1109    0.0200    0.0183
%      0.0200    0.0372    0.0269
%      0.0183    0.0269    0.0420

F=inv(C)*M % Kelly optimal leverages
```

```
% F =
%
%      1.2919
%      1.1723
%     -1.4882
```

Notice that the mean excess return of RTH is negative. Given this, it is not surprising that the Kelly formula recommends we short RTH.

You might wonder what the Sharpe ratio and the maximum compounded growth rate generated using this optimal allocation are. It turns out that the maximum growth rate of a multistrategy Gaussian process is

$$g(F^*) = r + F^{*T}CF^*/2$$

and the Sharpe ratio is given by

$$S = \sqrt{F^{*T}CF^*}$$

Here is the MATLAB code snippet that calculates these two quantities:

```
% Maximum annualized compounded growth rate
g=0.04+F'*C*F/2 % g =
%
%      0.1529

S=sqrt(F'*C*F) % Sharpe ratio of portfolio
% S =
%
%      0.4751
```

Notice that the compounded growth rate of the portfolio is 15.29 percent, higher than that of the maximum growth rate achievable by any of the individual stocks. (As an exercise, you can verify that the compounded growth rate of OIH, which has the highest one-period return among the three stocks, is 12.78 percent.)

Note that following the Kelly formula requires you to continuously adjust your capital allocation as your equity changes so that it remains optimal. Based on the SPY example (6.2), let's say you followed the Kelly formula and bought a portfolio worth $252,800. The next day, disaster struck, and you lost 10 percent on the SPY. So now your portfolio is worth only $227,520, and your equity is now only $74,720. What should you do now? Kelly's criterion will dictate that you immediately reduce the size of your portfolio to $188,892. Why? Because the optimal leverage of 2.528 times the current equity of $74,720 is $188,892.

As a practical procedure, this continuous updating of the capital allocation should occur at least once at the end of each trading day. In addition to updating the capital allocation, one should also periodically update F^* itself by recalculating the most recent trailing mean return and standard deviation. What should the lookback period be and how often do you need to update these inputs to the Kelly formula? These depend on the average holding period of your strategy. If you hold your positions for only one day or so, then as a rule of thumb, I would advise using a lookback period of six months. Using a relatively short lookback period has the advantage of allowing you to gradually reduce your exposure to strategies that have been losing their performance. As for the frequency of update, it should not be a burden to update F^* daily once you have written a program to do so.

One last point: Some strategies generate a variable number of trading signals each day, which may result in a variable number of positions and thus total capital each day. How should the Kelly formula be used to determine the capital in this case when we don't know what it will be beforehand? One can still use the Kelly formula to determine the *maximum* number of positions and thus the maximum capital allowed. It is always safer to have a leverage below what the Kelly formula recommends.

RISK MANAGEMENT

We saw in the previous section that the Kelly formula is not only useful for the optimal allocation of capital and for the determination of the optimal leverage, but also for risk management. In fact, the SPY example (6.2) illustrated that the Kelly formula would advise you to reduce the portfolio size in the face of trading losses. This selling at a loss is the frequent result of risk management, whether or not the risk management scheme is based on Kelly's formula.

Risk management always dictates that you should reduce your position size whenever there is a loss, even when it means realizing those losses. (The other face of the coin is that optimal leverage dictates that you should increase your position size when your strategy generates profits.) This kind of selling is believed by some analysts to be the cause of "financial contagion" affecting many large hedge funds simultaneously when one faces a large loss.

An example of this is the summer 2007 meltdown, described in the previously cited article "What Happened to the Quants in August 2007?" by Amir Khandani and Andrew Lo. During August 2007, under the ominous cloud of a housing and mortgage default crisis, a number of well-known hedge funds experienced unprecedented losses, with Goldman Sachs's Global Alpha fund falling 22.5 percent. Several billion dollars evaporated within all of one week. Even Renaissance Technologies Corporation, arguably the most successful quantitative hedge fund of all time, lost 8.7 percent in the first half of August, though it later recovered most of it. Not only is the magnitude of the loss astounding, but the widespread nature of it was causing great concern in the financial community. Strangest of all, few of these funds hold any mortgage-backed securities at all, ostensibly the root cause of the panic. It therefore became a classic study of financial contagion as propagated by hedge funds.

This kind of contagion occurs because a large loss by one hedge fund causes it to sell off some large positions that it holds (whether or not these are the positions that cause the loss in the first place). This selling causes the prices of the securities to drop (or rise in the case of short positions). If other hedge funds are holding similar positions, they will then suffer large losses also, causing their own risk management system to sell off their own positions, and on and on. For example, in the summer of 2007, one large hedge fund might have been holding subprime mortgage-backed securities and suffered a large loss in that sector. Risk management then required that it sold off liquid stock positions in their portfolio which might, up to that point, be unaffected by the subprime debacle. Because of the selling of such stock positions, other statistical arbitrage hedge funds that hold no mortgage-backed securities might now suffered big losses, and proceeded to sell their stocks as well. Hence, a sell-off in the mortgage-backed securities market suddenly became a sell-off in the stock market—a nice demonstration of the meaning of *contagion*.

Given the necessity of realizing losses as well as the scale and frequency of trading required to constantly rebalance the portfolio in order to closely follow the Kelly formula, it is understandable that most traders prefer to trade at half-Kelly leverage. A lower leverage implies a smaller size of the selling required for risk management.

Sometimes, even taking the conservative half-Kelly formula may be too aggressive, and traders may want to limit their portfolio size further by additional constraints. This is because, as I pointed out previously, the application of the Kelly formula to continuous finance is premised on the assumption that return distribution is Gaussian. (Finance is continuous in the sense that the outcomes of making bets in the financial market fall on a continuum of profits or losses, as opposed to a game of cards where the outcomes fall into discrete cases.) But, of course, the returns are not really Gaussian: large losses occur at far higher frequencies than would be predicted by a nice bell-shaped curve. Some people refer to the true distributions of returns as having "fat tails." What this means is that the probability of an event far, far away from the mean is much higher than allowed by the Gaussian bell curve. These highly improbable events have been called "black swan" events by the author Nassim Taleb (see Taleb, 2007).

To handle extreme events that fall outside the Gaussian distribution, we can use our simple backtest technique to roughly estimate what the maximum one-period loss was historically. (The period may be one week, one day, or one hour. The only criterion to use is that you should be ready to rebalance your portfolio according to the Kelly formula at the end of every period.) You should also have in mind what is the maximum one-period drawdown on your equity that you are willing to suffer. Dividing the maximum tolerable one-period drawdown on equity by the maximum historical loss will tell you whether even half-Kelly leverage is too large for your comfort. The leverage to use is always the smaller of the half-Kelly leverage and the maximum leverage obtained using the worst historical loss. In the S&P 500 index example in the previous section, the maximum historical one-day loss is about 20.47 percent, which occurred on October 19, 1987—"Black Monday." If you can tolerate only a 20 percent one-day drawdown on equity, then the maximum leverage you can apply is about 1. Meanwhile, the leverage recommended by half-Kelly is 1.26. Hence, in this case, even half-Kelly leverage would *not* be conservative enough to survive Black Monday.

The truly scary scenario in risk management is the one that has not occurred in history before. Echoing the philosopher Ludwig Wittgenstein, "Whereof one cannot speak, thereof one must be silent"—on such unknowables, theoretical models are appropriately silent.

IS THE USE OF STOP LOSS A GOOD RISK MANAGEMENT PRACTICE?

Some traders believe that good risk management means imposing stop loss on every trade; that is, if a position incurs a certain percent loss, the trader will exit the position. It is a common fallacy to believe that imposing stop loss will prevent the portfolio from suffering catastrophic losses. When a catastrophic event occurs, securities prices will drop discontinuously, so the stop loss orders to exit the positions will only be filled at prices much worse than those before the event. So, by exiting the positions, we are actually realizing the catastrophic loss and not avoiding it. For stop loss to be beneficial, we must believe that we are in a momentum, or trending, regime. In other words, we must believe that the prices will get worse within the expected lifetime of our trade. Otherwise, if the market is mean reverting within that lifetime, we will eventually recoup our losses if we didn't exit the position too quickly.

Of course, it is not easy to tell whether one is in a momentum regime (when stop loss is beneficial) or in a mean-reverting regime (when stop loss is harmful). My own observation is that when the movement of prices is due to news or other fundamental reasons (such as a company's deteriorating revenue), one is likely to be in a momentum regime, and one should not "stand in front of a freight train," in traders' vernacular. For example, if a fundamental analysis of a company reveals that it is currently overvalued, its stock price will likely gradually decrease (at least in relation to the market index) in order to reach a new, lower equilibrium price. This movement to the lower equilibrium price is irreversible as long as the fundamental economics of the company does not change. However, when securities prices move drastically without any apparent news or reasons, it is likely that the move is the result of a liquidity event—for example, major holders of the securities suddenly need to liquidate large positions for their own idiosyncratic reasons, or major speculators suddenly decide to cover their short positions. These liquidity events are of relatively short durations and mean reversion to the previous price levels is likely.

I will discuss in some more detail the appropriate exit strategies for mean-reverting versus momentum strategies in Chapter 7.

Beyond position risk (which is comprised of both market risk and specific risk), there are other forms of risks to consider: model risk, software risk, and natural disaster risk, in decreasing order of likelihood.

Model risk simply refers to the possibility that trading losses are not due to the statistical vagaries of the market, but to the fact that the trading model is wrong. It could be wrong for a large number of reasons, some of which were detailed in Chapter 3: data-snooping bias, survivorship bias, and so on. To eliminate all these different biases and errors in the backtest programs, it is extremely helpful to have a collaborator or consultant to duplicate your backtest results independently to ensure their validity. This need to duplicate results is routinely done in scientific research and is no less essential in financial research.

Model risk can also come not from any bias or error in your model or backtesting procedure, but from increased competition from other institutional traders all running the same strategy as you; or it could be a result of some fundamental change in market structure that eliminated the edge of your trading model. This is the regime shift that I talked about in Chapter 5.

There is not much you can do to alleviate these sources of model risk, except to gradually lower the leverage of the model as it racks up losses, up to the point where the leverage is zero. This can be accomplished in a systematic way if you constantly update the leverage according to the Kelly formula based on the trailing mean return and standard deviation. (As the mean return decreases to zero in the lookback period, your Kelly leverage will be driven to zero.) This is preferable to abruptly shutting down a model because of a large drawdown (see my discussion of the psychological pressure to shut down models prematurely in the following section on psychological preparedness).

Software risk refers to the case where the automated trading system that generates trades every day actually does not faithfully reflect your backtest model. This happens because of the omnipresent software bugs. I discussed the way to eliminate such software errors in Chapter 5: you should compare the trades generated by your automated trading system with the theoretical trades generated by your backtest system to ensure that they are the same.

Finally, physical or natural disasters can happen, which can cause big losses, and they don't have to be anything dramatic like earthquakes or tsunami. What if your Internet connection went down before you could enter a hedging position? What if your power went down in the middle of transmitting a trade? The different methods of preventing physical disasters from causing major disruptions to your trading can be found in the section on physical infrastructure in Chapter 4.

PSYCHOLOGICAL PREPAREDNESS

It may seem strange that a book on quantitative trading would include a section on psychological preparedness. After all, isn't quantitative trading supposed to liberate us from our emotions and let the computer make all the trading decisions in a disciplined manner? If only it were this easy: human traders who are not psychologically prepared will often override their automated trading systems' decisions, especially when there is a position or day with abnormal profit or loss. Hence, it is critical even if we trade using quantitative strategies to understand some of our own psychological weaknesses.

Fortunately, there is a field of financial research called "behavioral finance" (Thaler, 1994) that studies irrational financial decision making. I will try to highlight a few of the common irrational behaviors that affect trading.

The first behavioral bias is known variously as the *endowment effect*, *status quo bias*, or *loss aversion*. The first two effects cause some traders to hold on to a losing position for too long, because traders (and people in general) give too much preference to the status quo (the status quo bias), or because they demand much more to give up the stock than what they would pay to acquire it (the endowment effect). As I argued in the risk management section, there are rational reasons to hold on to a losing position (e.g., when you expect mean-reverting behavior); however, these behavioral biases cause traders to hold on to losing positions even when there is no rational reason (e.g., when you expect trending behavior, and the trend is such that your positions will lose even more). At the same time, the loss aversion bias causes some traders to exit their profitable positions too soon, even if holding longer will lead to a larger profit on average. Why do they exit the profitable positions so soon? Because the pain from possibly losing some of the current profits outweighs the pleasure from gaining higher profits.

This behavioral bias manifests itself most clearly and most disastrously when one has entered a position by mistake (because of either a software bug, an operational error, or a data problem) and has incurred a big loss. The rational step to take is to exit the position immediately upon discovery of the error. However, traders are often tempted to wait for mean reversion such that the loss is smaller before they exit. Unless you have a model for mean reversion that suggests now is a good time to enter into this position, this wait for mean reversion may very well lead to bigger losses instead.

Another common bias that I have personally experienced is the "representativeness bias"—people tend to put too much weight on recent experience and underweight long-term average (Ritter, 2003). (This reference has a good introduction to various biases studied by behavioral finance.) After a big loss, traders—even quantitative traders—tend to immediately modify certain parameters of their strategies so that they would have avoided the big loss if they were to trade this modified system. But, of course, this is unwise because this modification may invite some other big loss that is yet to happen, or it may have eliminated many profit opportunities that existed. We must remember that we are operating in a probabilistic regime: No system can avoid all the market vagaries that can result in losses.

If you feel that your system really is deficient and want to tweak it, you should always backtest the modified version to make sure that it does outperform the old system over a sufficiently long back-test period, not just over the last few weeks.

There are two major psychological weaknesses that are more well known to the traders than to economists: despair and greed.

Despair occurs when a trading model is in a major, prolonged drawdown. Many traders (and their managers, investors, etc.) will be under great pressure under this circumstance to shut down the model completely. Other overly self-confident traders with a reckless bent will do the opposite: They will double their bets on their losing models, hoping to recoup their losses eventually, if and when the models rebound. Neither behavior is rational: if you have been managing your capital allocation and leverage by the Kelly formula, you would lower the capital allocation for the losing model gradually.

Greed is the more usual emotion when the model is having a good run and is generating a lot of profits. The temptation now is to increase its leverage quickly in order to get rich quickly. Once again, a well-disciplined quantitative trader will keep the leverage below the dictates of the Kelly formula as well as the caution imposed by the possibility of fat-tail events.

Both despair and greed can lead to overleveraging (i.e., trading an overly large portfolio): In despair, one tries to recoup the losses by adding fresh capital; in greed, one adds capital too quickly after initial successes with a strategy. Therefore, the one golden rule in risk management is to keep the size of your portfolio under control at all times. This is, however, easier said than done. Large, well-known funds have succumbed to the temptation to overleverage and failed: Long-Term Capital Management in 2000 (Lowenstein, 2000) and Amaranth Advisors in 2006 (epchan. blogspot.com/2006/10/highly-improbable-event.html). In the Amaranth Advisors case, the leverage employed on one single strategy (natural gas calendar spread trade) due to one single trader (Brian Hunter) is so large that a $6 billion dollar loss was incurred, comfortably wiping out the fund's equity—a textbook case of risk mismanagement.

I have experienced this pressure myself both in an institutional setting and in a personal setting, and the unfortunate result both times was to succumb prematurely. When I was with a money management firm, I lost over $1 million for the fund's investors because, in a fit of greed, I added over $100 million to a portfolio based on a strategy that had been traded for barely six months. (That was before I learned of the Kelly criterion.) As if this is not enough lesson, I repeated the same mistake again when I started trading independently. It concerns a mean-reverting spread strategy involving XLE, an energy exchange-traded fund (ETF) and the crude oil future (CL). When the spread refused to mean revert over time, I stubbornly increased the size of the spread to almost $500,000. Finally, despair set in, and I exited the spread with close to a six-figure loss. Naturally, the spread started to revert afterward when I wasn't around to benefit. (Fortunately, several of my other strategies performed well in that first year of my independent trading, so the fiscal year ended with only a small overall loss.)

How should we train ourselves to overcome these psychological weaknesses and learn not to override the models manually and to remedy trading errors correctly and expeditiously? As with most human endeavors, the way to do this is to start with a small portfolio and gradually gain psychological preparedness, discipline, and confidence in your models. As you become emotionally more able to handle the daily swings in profit and loss (P&L) and rein in the primordial urges of the psyche, your portfolio's actual performance will hew to the theoretically expected performance of your strategy.

I have certainly found that to be the case after getting over those aforementioned disastrous trades. My newfound discipline and faith in the Kelly formula has so far prevented similar disasters from happening again.

SUMMARY

Risk management is a crucial discipline in trading. The trading world is littered with numerous examples of giant hedge funds and investment banks laid low by enormous losses due to a single trade or in a very short period of time. Most of these losses are due to overleveraging positions and not to an inherently erroneous model. Typically, traders will not overleverage a model that has not worked very well. It is a hitherto superbly performing model that is at the greatest risk of huge loss due to overconfidence and overleverage. This chapter therefore provides an important tool for risk management: the determination of the optimal leverage using the Kelly formula.

Besides the determination of the optimal leverage, the Kelly formula has a very useful side benefit: It also determines the optimal allocation of capital among different strategies, based on the covariance of their returns.

But no risk management formula or system will prevent disasters if you are not psychologically prepared for the ups and downs of trading and thus deviating from the prescriptions of rational decision making (i.e., your models). The ultimate risk management mind-set is very simple: Do not succumb to either despair or greed. To gain practice in this psychological discipline, one must proceed slowly with small position size, and thoroughly test various aspects of the trading business (model, software, operational procedure, money and risk management) before scaling up according to the Kelly formula.

I have found that in order to proceed slowly and cautiously, it is helpful to have other sources of income or other businesses to help sustain yourself either financially or emotionally (to avoid the boredom associated with slow progress). It is indeed possible that finding a diversion, whether income producing or not, may actually help improve the long-term growth of your wealth.

APPENDIX: A SIMPLE DERIVATION OF THE KELLY FORMULA WHEN RETURN DISTRIBUTION IS GAUSSIAN

If we assume that the return distribution of a strategy (or security) is Gaussian, then the Kelly formula can be derived very easily. We start with the formula for a compounded, levered growth rate applicable to a Gaussian process:

$$g(f) = r + fm - s^2 f^2/2$$

where f is the leverage, r is the risk-free rate; m is the average simple, uncompounded one-period excess return; and s is the standard deviation of those uncompounded returns. This formula for compounded growth rate can itself be derived quite simply, but not as simply as the Kelly formula, so I leave its derivation for the reader to look up in the Thorp article referenced earlier.

To find the optimal f which maximizes g, simply take its first derivative with respect to f and set the derivative to zero:

$$dg/df = m - s^2 f = 0$$

Solving this equation for f gives us $f = m/s^2$, the Kelly formula for one strategy or security under the Gaussian assumption.

CHAPTER 7

Special Topics in Quantitative Trading

T he first six chapters of this book covered most of the basic knowledge needed to research, develop, and execute your own quantitative strategy. This chapter explains important themes in quantitative trading in more detail. These themes form the bases of statistical arbitrage trading, and most quantitative traders are conversant in some if not most of these topics. They are also very helpful in informing our intuition about trading.

I will describe the two basic categories of trading strategies: mean-reverting versus momentum strategies. Periods of mean-reverting and trending behaviors are examples of what some traders call *regimes*, and the switch between different regimes is a topic of discussion here. Mean-reverting strategies derive their mathematical justification from the concepts of stationarity and cointegration of time series, which I will cover next. Then I will describe a theory that many hedge funds use to manage large portfolios and one that has caused much turmoil in their performances: namely, factor models. Other categories of strategies that traders frequently discuss are seasonal trading and high-frequency strategies. All trading strategies require a way to exit their positions; I will describe the different logical ways to do this. Finally, I ponder the question of how to best enhance the returns of a strategy: through higher leverage or trading higher-beta stocks?

MEAN-REVERTING VERSUS
MOMENTUM STRATEGIES

Trading strategies can be profitable only if securities prices are either mean-reverting or trending. Otherwise, they are random-walking, and trading will be futile. If you believe that prices are mean reverting and that they are currently low relative to some reference price, you should buy now and plan to sell higher later. However, if you believe the prices are trending and that they are currently low, you should (short) sell now and plan to buy at an even lower price later. The opposite is true if you believe prices are high.

Academic research has indicated that stock prices are *on average* very close to random walking. However, this does not mean that under certain special conditions, they cannot exhibit some degree of mean reversion or trending behavior. Furthermore, at any given time, stock prices can be both mean reverting and trending depending on the time horizon you are interested in. Constructing a trading strategy is essentially a matter of determining if the prices under certain conditions and for a certain time horizon will be mean reverting or trending, and what the initial reference price should be at any given time. (When the prices are trending, they are also said to have "momentum," and thus the corresponding trading strategy is often called a *momentum strategy*.)

Some people like to describe the phenomenon that prices can be both mean reverting and trending at the same time as the "fractal" nature of stock prices. Technical analysts or chartists like to use the so-called Elliott wave theory to analyze such phenomena. Still others like to use the discipline of machine learning or artificial intelligence (in particular, techniques such as hidden Markov models, Kalman filter, neural networks, etc.) to discover whether the prices are in a mean-reverting or trending "regime." I personally have not found such general theories of mean reversion or momentum particularly useful. (See, however, the section on regime switching, which describes an apparently successful attempt to predict regime switch for one particular stock.) Rather, I find it is usually safe to assume that, unless the expected earnings of a company have changed, stock prices will be mean reverting. In fact, financial researchers (Khandani and Lo, 2007) have constructed a very simple short-term mean reversal model that is profitable (before transaction costs) over many years. Of course, whether the mean reversion is strong enough and consistent enough such that we can trade profitably after factoring in transaction costs is another matter, and it is up to you, the trader, to find those special circumstances when it is strong and consistent.

Though mean reversion is quite prevalent, backtesting a profitable mean-reverting strategy can be quite perilous.

Many historical financial databases contain errors in price quotes. Any such error tends to artificially inflate the performance of mean-reverting strategies. It is easy to see why: a mean-reverting strategy will buy on a fictitious quote that is much lower than some moving average and sell on the next correct quote that is in line with the moving average and thus makes a profit. One must make sure the data is thoroughly cleansed of such fictitious quotes before one can completely trust your backtesting performance on a mean-reverting strategy.

Survivorship bias also affects the backtesting of mean-reverting strategies disproportionately, as I discussed in Chapter 3. Stocks that went through extreme price actions are likely to be either acquired (the prices went very high) or went bankrupt (the prices went to zeros). A mean-reverting strategy will short the former and buy the latter, losing money in both cases. However, these stocks may not appear at all in your historical database if it has survivorship bias, thus artificially inflating your backtest performance. You can look up Table 3.1 to find out which database has survivorship bias.

Momentum can be generated by the slow diffusion of information—as more people become aware of certain news, more people decide to buy or sell a stock, thereby driving the price in the same direction. I suggested earlier that stock prices may exhibit momentum when the expected earnings have changed. This can happen when a company announces its quarterly earnings, and investors either gradually become aware of this announcement or they react to this change by incrementally executing a large order (so as to minimize market impact). And indeed, this leads to a momentum strategy called *post earnings announcement drift*, or PEAD. (For a particularly useful article with lots of references on this strategy, look up quantlogic.blogspot.com/2006/03/pocket-phd-post-earning-announcment.html.) Essentially, this strategy recommends that you buy a stock when its earnings exceed expectations, and short a stock when it falls short. More generally, many news announcements have the potential of altering expectations of a stock's future earnings, and therefore have the potential to trigger a trending period. As to what kind of news will trigger this, and how long the trending period will last, it is again up to you to find out.

Besides the slow diffusion of information, momentum can be caused by the incremental execution of a large order due to the liquidity needs or private investment decisions of a large investor. This cause probably accounts for more instances of short-term momentum than any other causes. With the advent of increasingly sophisticated execution algorithms adopted by the large brokerages, it is, however, increasingly difficult to ascertain whether a large order is behind the observed momentum.

Momentum can also be generated by the herdlike behavior of investors: investors interpret the (possibly random and meaningless) buying or selling decisions of others as the sole justifications of their own trading decisions. As Yale economist Robert Schiller said in the *New York Times* (Schiller, 2008), nobody has all the information they need in order to make a fully informed financial decision. One has to rely on the judgment of others. There is, however, no sure way to discern the quality of the judgment of others. More problematically, people make their financial decisions at different times, not meeting at a town hall and reaching a consensus once and for all. The first person who paid a high price for a house is "informing" the others that houses are good investments, which leads another person to make the same decision, and so on. Thus, a possibly erroneous decision by the first buyer is propagated as "information" to a herd of others.

Unfortunately, momentum regimes generated by these two causes (private liquidity needs and herdlike behavior) have highly unpredictable time horizons. How could you know how big an order an institution needs to execute incrementally? How do you predict when the "herd" is large enough to form a stampede? Where is the infamous tipping point? If we do not have a reliable way to estimate these time horizons, we cannot execute a momentum trade profitably based on these phenomena. In a later section on regime switch, I will examine some attempts to predict these tipping or "turning" points.

There is one last contrast between mean-reverting and momentum strategies that is worth pondering. What are the effects of increasing competition from traders with the same strategies? For mean-reverting strategies, the effect typically is the gradual elimination of any arbitrage opportunity, and thus gradually diminishing returns down to zero. When the number of arbitrage opportunities has been reduced to almost zero, the mean-reverting strategy is subject to the risk that an increasing percentage of trading signals are actually due to fundamental changes in stocks' valuation and thus is not going to mean revert. For momentum strategies, the effect of competition is often the diminishing of the time horizon over which the trend will continue. As news disseminates at a faster rate and as more traders take advantage of this trend earlier on, the equilibrium price will be reached sooner. Any trade entered after this equilibrium price is reached will be unprofitable.

REGIME SWITCHING*

The concept of regimes is most basic to financial markets. What else are "bull" and "bear" markets if not regimes? The desire to predict regime switches, which are also commonly known as *turning points*, is also as old as financial markets themselves.

If our attempts to predict the switching from a bull to a bear market were even slightly successful, we could focus our

---

*This section was adapted from an article I published in *Automated Trader* magazine.

QUANTITATIVE TRADING

120

discussion to this one type of switching and call it a day. If only it were that easy. The difficulty with predicting this type of switching encourages researchers to look more broadly at other types of regime switching in the financial markets, hoping to find some that may be more amenable to existing statistical tools.

I have already described two regime switches (or "shifts," for these two examples did not switch back to their former regimes) that are due to changes in market and regulatory structures: decimalization of stock prices in 2003 and the elimination of the short-sale plus-tick rule in 2007. (See Chapter 5 for details.) These regime shifts are preannounced by the government, so no predictions of the shifts are necessary, though few people can predict the exact consequences of the regulatory changes.

Some of the other most common financial or economic regimes studied are inflationary vs. recessionary regimes, high- vs. low-volatility regimes, and mean-reverting vs. trending regimes. Among these, volatility regime switching seems to be most amenable to classical econometric tools such as the generalized autoregressive conditional heteroskedasticity (GARCH) model (See Klaassen, 2002). That is not surprising, as there is a long history of success among financial economists in modeling volatilities as opposed to the underlying stock prices themselves. While such predictions of volatility regime switches can be of great value to options traders, they are unfortunately of no help to stock traders.

Academic attempts to model regime switches in stock prices generally proceed along these lines:

1. Propose that the two (or more) regimes are characterized by different probability distributions of the prices. In the simplest cases, the log of the prices of both regimes may be represented by normal distributions, except that they have different means and/or standard deviations.

2. Assume that there is some kind of transition probability among the regimes.

3. Determine the exact parameters that specify the regime probability distributions and the transition probabilities by fitting the

model to past prices, using standard statistical methods such as maximum likelihood estimation.

4. Based on the fitted model above, find out the expected regime of the next time step and, more importantly, the expected stock price.

This type of approach is usually called *Markov regime switching* or *hidden Markov models*, and it is generally based on a Bayesian probabilistic framework. Readers who are interested in reading more about some of these approaches may peruse Nielsen and Olesen (2000), van Norden and Schaller (1993), or Kaufmann and Scheicher (1996).

Despite the elegant theoretical framework, such Markov regime-switching models are generally useless for actual trading purposes. The reason for this weakness is that they assume constant transition probabilities among regimes at all times. In practice, this means that at any time (as illustrated by the Nielsen and Olesen paper), there is always a very small probability for the stock to transition from a normal, quiescent regime to a volatile regime. But this is useless to traders who want to know when—and under what precise conditions—the transition probability will suddenly peak. This question is tackled by the turning points models.

Turning points models take a data mining approach (Chai, 2007): Enter all possible variables that might predict a turning point or regime switch. Variables such as current volatility; last-period return; or changes in macroeconomic numbers such as consumer confidence, oil price changes, bond price changes, and so on can all be part of this input. In fact, in a very topical article about turning points in the real estate market by economist Robert Schiller (2007), it was suggested that the crescendo of media chatter about impending boom or bust may actually be a good predictor of a coming turning point.

In Example 7.1, I illustrate how we might detect turning points using a data-mining approach with just simple technical indicators built on stock price series as inputs while using stock returns of multiple holding periods as outputs.

Example 7.1: Using a Machine Learning Tool to Profit from Regime Switching in the Stock Market

As I discussed in the main text, I believe that regime switching can be most easily discovered by using a data-mining approach: examining a massive number of indicators to see which one might predict a switch. This is normally a very onerous task, even with MATLAB. But, luckily, a recent machine learning program has enabled this discovery process to be done in a matter of hours.

I shall employ a tool here called Alphacet Discovery, which is an integrated backtesting and execution platform recently launched by Alphacet, Inc. (www.alphacet.com. Full disclosure: Alphacet is a client of my firm.) This platform not only integrates all historical and real-time data needed for rapid strategy prototyping, backtesting, analysis, and real-time deployment; it also contains an expanding array of machine learning programs such as neural networks and genetic algorithms that are well suited to data mining for the kind of relationships we are seeking.

I will pick a prominent brokerage stock—GS—as a proxy for the financial sector. My objective is to find out if I can detect turning points in this sector where it goes from bull to bear and back. My initial hypothesis is that major shifts of interest rates, a release of government macroeconomic data, or earnings announcements are likely triggers of turning points. At the time of this writing, Alphacet had not yet completed integration of macroeconomic or company news data into its database, so I will use a large percent change in GS as proxy for such news releases. Furthermore, I believe that whenever GS reaches an N-day high or low just before this large drop or rise in prices occurs is a good signal that a previous regime is close to an end. So I shall use this condition as an additional input as well.

The search problem we face is: How large a percent change is sufficient to trigger a regime switch? What should N be in the N-day high/low condition? And how long does the new regime generally last? (In other words, what is the optimal holding period?) To answer these questions in the old-fashioned, manual way is very time consuming, as one has to run multiple simulations with different thresholds for the independent variables and multiple return horizons for the dependent variables. Let's see if Alphacet Discovery can help us automate this process.

The independent variables of the model are just the one-day returns of GS. The dependent variables are the future returns of GS within various holding periods. Discovery can easily find an optimal rule, or an optimal combination of rules, which will lead to the best backtest performance. In our case, each percent-change threshold can be encapsulated as a rule. I entered two thresholds for buys and two for shorts: −1 percent, −3 percent,

1 percent, and 3 percent. Similarly, each holding period can be encapsulated as a rule, too, and I entered six such periods: 1, 5, 10, 20, 40, and 60 days.

To prepare the price, percent-change, and 10-day high/low time series for this search is very easy: most things can be done by drag and drop, using a mouse, in Discovery. (For simplicity, I fix *N* to 10 for the strategy here, but this parameter can be optimized as well.) I just dragged a GS price series into the strategy editor and specified a 1-day frequency with the available controls. (The price series started around December 2006.) See box S1 in Figure 7.1. Then I dragged several prepackaged "Rules" that compute the 1-day percent change, and simple 10-day moving highs and lows of a series to the strategy editor (box I2 in Figure 7.1.). And I feed the original price series into the Program Group box by directing an arrow from the Symbol Group box to the Program Group box.

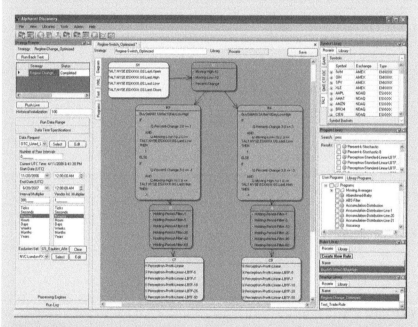

FIGURE 7.1 Strategy Editor Showing Data and Rules Represented by Boxes

Now I can create the entry rules by using the drop-down menus and typing into the textboxes inside a new Rule box's editor. Figure 7.2 shows what's inside Rule box R3 for the buy-and-sell rule based on a change of ±1 percent. I have created a similar Rule box for ±3 percent. Note that, by default, subsequent entry signals will override positions established by previous signals.

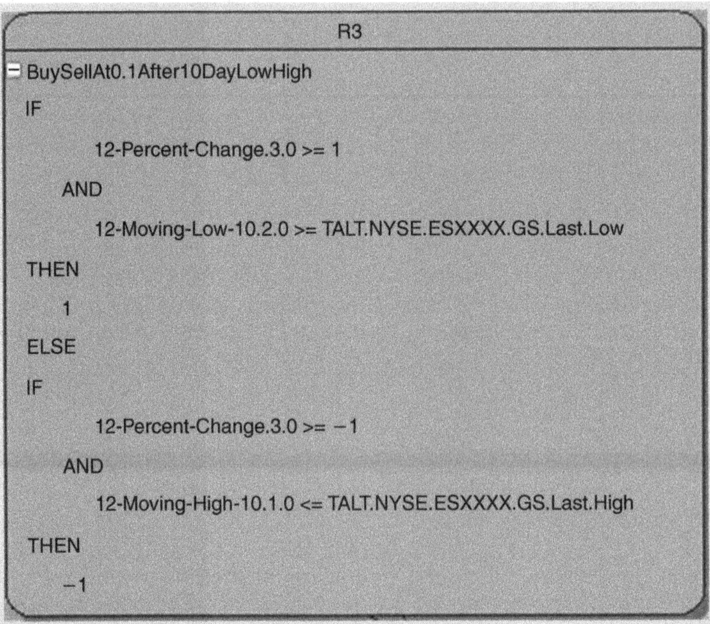

```
                              R3
⊟ BuySellAt0.1After10DayLowHigh
   IF
           12-Percent-Change.3.0 >= 1
       AND
           12-Moving-Low-10.2.0 >= TALT.NYSE.ESXXXX.GS.Last.Low
   THEN
       1
   ELSE
   IF
           12-Percent-Change.3.0 >= −1
       AND
           12-Moving-High-10.1.0 <= TALT.NYSE.ESXXXX.GS.Last.High
   THEN
       −1
```

FIGURE 7.2   Inside a Rule Box

We can specify the holding periods using the prepackaged program called "Holding Period" with different parameters. (In fact, you can easily create such programs yourself if you know the programming language Lisp.) These are all encapsulated in the box I5 (and I6 for the ±2 percent rule separately). We feed the output of the boxes R3 to I5 by drawing an arrow, and similarly R4 to I9.

Finally, we run a perceptron learning algorithm on the outputs of I7 and I9 (a perceptron is a type of neural network). This algorithm will find out the best weights for the different rules with different holding periods (among other parameters) based on a moving window of historical training data with the objective of maximizing the total profit in this window. Based on these optimized weights, the perceptron will trigger a buy-and-sell decision at the end of each period. (Examples of other algorithms that you can select are genetic algorithm and a K-nearest-neighbor clustering technique.)

Interestingly, the perceptron will not force us to hold a position for exactly N days, even though that was what the component rule was constructed to do so in the moving window. Every day, the strategy will decide whether to buy, sell, or do nothing, based on the latest parameter optimization using the latest data in the moving window and the resulting linearly weighted decisions from the different rules.

Now we are ready to look at the performance results of this strategy. We can bring up Discovery's charting application for this. In Figure 7.3, I have shown three of the best equity curves that come from the perceptron optimization. The best curve belongs to a model using a 50-day moving window for the optimization. (The length of the moving window can itself be an object of optimization, but we will skip that step here.) On the side-bar of the charting application, we can see that this strategy has a 37.93 percent gross cumulative return over a six-month backtest period, with 89 round-trip trades. (This is to be compared with a 15.77 percent return of a buy-and-hold strategy on GS, with a 14 percent drawdown.) We have also shown the best equity curve from the various holding period routines to quantify the improvement from optimization (holding period of 10 days in I5 on the 1 percent rule at R3), which has a gross cumulative return of 18.55 percent over the period.

Though the backtest period is short, this return looks very impressive. Can something be wrong? In particular, what about the much-feared data-snooping bias that seems to creep into every strategy that is based on machine learning or artificial intelligence? The basic philosophy of Alphacet

FIGURE 7.3 Charting Application Showing Equity Curves and Performance Statistics in the Sidebar

Discovery is to prevent this kind of bias from happening. In theory, though not in our particular illustration here, optimization over all rules and all parameters can be done in a backward-looking moving window, so that we are using absolutely no unseen future data for the backtest. Of course, data-snooping bias can still creep in because we can abandon a whole category of models when the performance is poor and try one new category after another until it improves. But then, this is unavoidable whenever we are in the business of backtesting.

One should also note that the parameters that the search engine is allowed to optimize over in this case are actually quite limited: They are just the different holding periods. This further reduces the danger of data-snooping bias.

Since the backtest looks good, I can immediately press a single button and have this strategy run against real-time data and generate orders in either a paper or a real trading account.

As you can see, it may not be hard to create a regime-switching model with the simplest of technical indicators as long as one is able to efficiently optimize over a large number of parameters, conducted strictly in a backward-looking moving window. (See my sidebar on "Parameter-less Trading Models" in Chapter 3.) The performance may even be better if we can confirm the price moves with macroeconomic or company-specific news. I believe that this same technique can be applied profitably to many exchange-traded funds (ETFs), futures, or even currency trading as well.

I would like to thank Rosario Ingargiola, chief technology officer of Alphacet, Inc., for his help in using Alphacet Discovery to develop the strategy shown here.

STATIONARITY AND COINTEGRATION

A time series is "stationary" if it never drifts farther and farther away from its initial value. In technical terms, stationary time series are "integrated of order zero," or $I(0)$. (See Alexander, 2001.) It is obvious that if the price series of a security is stationary, it would be a great candidate for a mean-reversion strategy. Unfortunately, most stock price series are *not* stationary—they exhibit a geometric random walk that gets them farther and farther away from their starting (i.e., initial public offering) values. However, you can often find a pair of stocks such that if you long one and short the other, the market value of the pair is stationary. If this is the case, then the two individual time series are said to be *cointegrated*. They are so described because a linear combination of them is integrated of order zero. Typically, two stocks that form a cointegrating pair are from the same industry group. Traders have long been familiar with this so-called pair-trading strategy. They buy the pair portfolio when the spread of the stock prices formed by these pairs is low, and sell/short the pair when the spread is high—in other words, a classic mean-reverting strategy.

An example of a pair of cointegrating price series is the gold ETF GLD versus the gold miners ETF, GDX, which I discussed in Example 3.6. If we form a portfolio with long 1 share of GLD and short 1.6766 share of GDX, the prices of the portfolio form a stationary time series (see Figure 7.4). The exact number of shares of GLD and GDX can be determined by a regression fit of the two component time series (see Example 7.2).

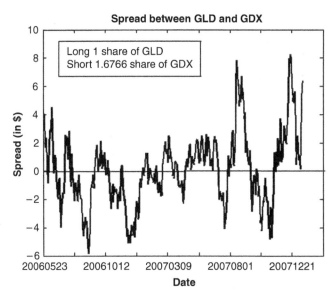

FIGURE 7.4 A Stationary Time Series Formed by the Spread between GLD and GDX

Example 7.2: How to Form a Good Cointegrating (and Mean-Reverting) Pair of Stocks

As I explained in the main text, if you long one security and short another one in the same industry group and in the right proportion, sometimes the combination (or "spread") becomes a stationary series. A stationary series is an excellent candidate for a mean-reverting strategy. This example teaches you how to use a free MATLAB package downloadable at www.spatial-econometrics.com to determine if two price series are cointegrated and, if so, how to find the optimal "hedge ratio" (i.e., the number of shares of the second security versus one share of the first security).

The main method used to test for cointegration is called the cointegrating augmented Dickey-Fuller test, hence the function name *cadf*. A detailed description of this method can be found in the manual also available on the same web site mentioned earlier.

The following program is available online as epchan.com/book/ example7_2.m:

```
% make sure previously defined variables are erased.
clear;
% read a spreadsheet named "GLD.xls" into MATLAB.
[num, txt]=xlsread('GLD');

% the first column (starting from the second row) is
% the trading days in format mm/dd/yyyy.
tday1=txt(2:end, 1);
% convert the format into yyyymmdd.
tday1=..
datestr(datenum(tday1, 'mm/dd/yyyy'), 'yyyymmdd');

% convert the date strings first into cell arrays and
% then into numeric format.
tday1=str2double(cellstr(tday1));
% the last column contains the adjusted close prices.
adjcls1=num(:, end);
% read a spreadsheet named "GDX.xls" into MATLAB.
[num2, txt2]=xlsread('GDX');
% the first column (starting from the second row) is
% the trading days in format mm/dd/yyyy.
tday2=txt2(2:end, 1);
% convert the format into yyyymmdd.
tday2=..
datestr(datenum(tday2, 'mm/dd/yyyy'), 'yyyymmdd');
```

```
% convert the date strings first into cell arrays and
% then into numeric format.
tday2=str2double(cellstr(tday2));
adjcls2=num2(:, end);

% find all the days when either GLD or GDX has data.
tday=union(tday1, tday2);
[foo idx idx1]=intersect(tday, tday1);

% combining the two price series
adjcls=NaN(length(tday), 2);
adjcls(idx, 1)=adjcls1(idx1);


[foo idx idx2]=intersect(tday, tday2);

adjcls(idx, 2)=adjcls2(idx2);

% days where any one price is missing
baddata=find(any(~isfinite(adjcls), 2));
tday(baddata)=[];

adjcls(baddata,:)=[];

vnames=strvcat('GLD', 'GDX');

% run cointegration check using
% augmented Dickey-Fuller test
res=cadf(adjcls(:, 1), adjcls(:, 2), 0, 1);
prt(res, vnames);

% Output from cadf function:

%  Augmented DF test for co-integration variables:
   GLD,GDX
% CADF t-statistic         # of lags    AR(1) estimate
%      -3.35698533                 1        -0.060892
%
%    1% Crit Value    5% Crit Value    10% Crit Value
%        -3.819          -3.343           -3.042

% The t-statistic of -3.36 which is in between the
% 1% Crit Value of -3.819
% and the 5% Crit Value of -3.343 means that
% there is a better than 95%
% probability that these 2 time series are
% cointegrated.
```

```
results=ols(adjcls(:, 1), adjcls(:, 2));

hedgeRatio=results.beta
z=results.resid;

% A hedgeRatio of 1.6766 was found.
% I.e. GLD=1.6766*GDX + z, where z can be
% interpreted as the
% spread GLD-1.6766*GDX and should be stationary.

% This should produce a chart similar to Figure 7.4.
plot(z);
```

In case you think that any two stocks in the same industry group would be cointegrating, here is a counterexample: KO (Coca-Cola) versus PEP (Pepsi). The same cointegration test as used in Example 7.1 tells us that there is a less than 90 percent probability that they are cointegrated. (You should try it yourself and then compare with my program epchan.com/book/example7_3.m.) If you use linear regression to find the best fit between KO and PEP, the plot of the time series will resemble Figure 7.5.

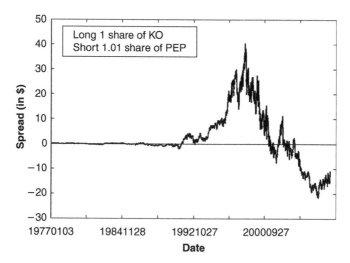

FIGURE 7.5 A Nonstationary Time Series Formed by the Spread between KO and PEP

If a price series (of a stock, a pair of stocks, or, in general, a portfolio of stocks) is stationary, then a mean-reverting strategy is guaranteed to be profitable, as long as the stationarity persists into the future (which is by no means guaranteed). However, the converse is not true. You don't necessarily need a stationary price series in order to have a successful mean-reverting strategy. Even a nonstationary price series can have many short-term reversal opportunities that one can exploit, as many traders have discovered.

Many pair traders are unfamiliar with the concepts of stationarity and cointegration. But most of them are familiar with *correlation*, which superficially seems to mean the same thing as cointegration. Actually, they are quite different. Correlation between two price series actually refers to the correlations of their returns over some time horizon (for concreteness, let's say a day). If two stocks are positively correlated, there is a good chance that their prices will move in the same direction most days. However, having a positive correlation does not say anything about the long-term behavior of the two stocks. In particular, it doesn't guarantee that the stock prices will not grow farther and farther apart in the long run even if they do move in the same direction most days. However, if two stocks were cointegrated and remain so in the future, their prices (weighted appropriately) will be unlikely to diverge. Yet their daily (or weekly, or any other time horizon) returns may be quite uncorrelated.

As an artificial example of two stocks, A and B, that are cointegrated but not correlated, see Figure 7.6. Stock B clearly doesn't move in any correlated fashion with stock A: Some days they move in the same direction, other days the opposite. Most days, stock B doesn't move at all. But notice that the spread in stock prices between A and B always returns to about $1 after a while.

Can we find real-life example of this phenomenon? Well, KO versus PEP is one. In the program example7_3.m I have shown that they do not cointegrate. If, however, you test their daily returns for correlation, you will find that their correlation of 0.4849 is indeed statistically significant. The correlation test is presented at the end of the example7_3.m program and shown here in Example 7.3.

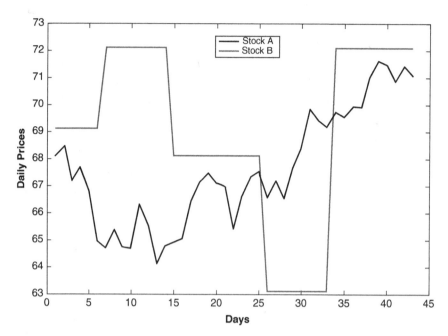

FIGURE 7.6 Cointegration Is Not Correlation. Stocks A and B are cointegrated but not correlated

---

Example 7.3: Testing the Cointegration versus Correlation Properties between KO and PEP

The cointegration test for KO and PEP is the same as that for GDX and GLD in Example 7.2, so it won't be repeated here. (It is available from epchan.com/book/example7_3.m) The cointegration result shows that the t-statistic for the augmented Dicky-Fuller test is −2.14, larger than the 10 percent critical value of −3.038, meaning that there is a less than 90 percent probability that these two time series are cointegrated.

The following code fragment, however, tests for correlation between the two time series:

```
% A test for correlation.
dailyReturns=(adjcls-lag1(adjcls))./lag1(adjcls);
[R,P]=corrcoef(dailyReturns(2:end,:));

% R =
%
%     1.0000    0.4849
%     0.4849    1.0000
```

```
%
%
%  P =
%
%        1      0
%        0      1

%  The P value of 0 indicates that the two time series
%  are significantly correlated.
```

Stationarity is not limited to the spread between stocks: it can also be found in certain currency rates. For example, the Canadian dollar/Australian dollar (CAD/AUD) cross-currency rate is quite stationary, both being commodities currencies. Numerous pairs of futures as well as well as fixed-income instruments can be found to be cointegrating as well. (The simplest examples of cointegrating futures pairs are calendar spreads: long and short futures contracts of the same underlying commodity but different expiration months. Similarly for fixed-income instruments, one can long and short bonds by the same issuer but of different maturities.)

FACTOR MODELS

Financial commentators often say something like this: "The current market favors value stocks," "The market is focusing on earnings growth," or "Investors are paying attention to inflation numbers." How do we quantify these and other common drivers of returns?

There is a well-known framework in quantitative finance called *factor models* (also known as arbitrage pricing theory [APT]) that attempts to capture the different drivers of returns such as earnings growth rates, interest rate, or the market capitalization of a company. These drivers are called *factors*. Mathematically, we can write the excess returns (returns minus risk-free rate) R of N stocks as

$$R = Xb + u$$

where X is an $N \times N$ matrix of factor exposures (also known as *factor loadings*), b is an N vector of factor returns, and u an N vector of specific returns. (Every one of these quantities is time dependent, but I suppress this explicit dependence for simplicity.)

The terms *factor exposure*, *factor return*, and *specific return* are commonly used in quantitative finance, and it is well worth our effort to understand their meanings. Factor returns are the common drivers of stock returns, and are therefore independent of a particular stock. Factor exposures are the sensitivities to each of these common drivers. Any part of a stock's return that cannot be explained by these common factor returns is deemed a specific return (i.e., specific to a stock and essentially regarded as just random noise within the APT framework). Each stock's specific return is assumed to be uncorrelated to another stock's.

Let's illustrate these using a simple factor model called the Fama-French Three-Factor model (Fama and French, 1992). This model postulates that the excess return of a stock depends linearly on only three factor exposures: its beta (i.e., its sensitivity to the market index), its market capitalization, and its book-to-price ratio. These factor exposures are obviously different for each stock and for each time period. (Factor exposures are often normalized such that the average of the factor exposures within a universe of stocks is zero, and the standard deviation is 1.)

Now that we know how to calculate the factor exposures, what about the factor returns and specific returns? We cannot directly compute the factor returns and specific returns—we have to infer their values by running a multivariate linear regression of the excess returns of stocks against the factor exposures. Note that each stock represents one data point in this linear regression, and we have to either run a separate linear regression for each time period or, if we want an average value over many time periods, aggregate the values from all these time periods into one training set and run one regression against them all.

If you perform this linear regression fit over many time periods for the Fama-French Three-Factor model, you will find that the market capitalization factor return is usually negative (meaning that small-cap stocks usually outperform large-cap stocks), and the book-to-price ratio factor return is usually positive (meaning value stocks usually outperform growth stocks). And since most stocks are positively correlated with the market index, the beta factor return is positive as well.

The Fama-French model has no monopoly on the choice of factors. In fact, you can construct as many factors as creativity and rationality allow. For example, you can choose return on equity as a factor exposure, or the correlation of the stock return with the prime rate as another. You can choose any number of other economic, fundamental, or technical factors. Whether the factor exposures you have chosen are sensible or not will determine whether the factor model explains the excess returns of the stocks adequately. If the factor exposures (and consequently the model as a whole) are poorly chosen, the linear regression fit will produce specific returns of significant sizes, and the R^2 statistic of the fit will be small. According to experts (Grinold and Kahn, 1999), the R^2 statistic of a good factor model with monthly returns of 1,000 stocks and 50 factors is typically about 30 percent to 40 percent.

It may appear that these factor models are only explanatory in retrospect—that is, given historical returns and factor exposures, we can compute the factor returns of those historical periods. But what good are those historical factor returns for our trading? It turns out that often factor returns are more stable than individual stock returns. In other words, they have *momentum*. You can therefore assume that their values remain unchanged from the current period (known from the regression fit) to the next time period. If this is the case, then, of course, you can also predict the excess returns, as long as the factor exposures are well chosen and therefore the time-varying specific returns are not significant.

Let me clarify one point of potential confusion. Even though I stated that factor models can be useful as a predictive model (and therefore for trading) only if we assume the factor returns have momentum, it does not mean that factor models cannot capture mean reversion of stock returns. You can, in fact, construct a factor exposure that captures mean reversion, such as the negative of the previous period return. If stock returns are indeed mean reverting, then the corresponding factor return will be positive.

If you are interested in building a trading model based on fundamental factors, there are a number of vendors from whom you can obtain historical factor data:

- Capital IQ: www.capitaliq.com
- Compustat: www.compustat.com
- MSCI Barra: www.mscibarra.com
- Northfield Information Services: www.northinfo.com
- Quantitative Services Group: www.qsg.com

Example 7.4: Principal Component Analysis as an Example of Factor Model

The examples of factor exposures I described above are typically economic (e.g., interest rates), fundamental (e.g., book-to-price ratio), or technical (e.g., previous period's return). To obtain historical values of these factor exposures for a large portfolio of stocks so as to backtest a factor model is usually quite expensive and not very practical to an independent trader. (For those who are fiscally prepared to purchase such data, see the list in the main text.) However, there is one kind of factor model that relies on nothing more than historical returns to construct. This method is the so-called principal component analysis (PCA).

If we use PCA to construct the factor exposures and factor returns, we must assume that the factor exposures are constant (time independent) over the estimation period. (This rules out factors that represent mean reversion or momentum, since these factor exposures depend on the prior period returns.) More importantly, we assume that the factor returns are *uncorrelated*; that is to say, their covariance matrix $\langle bb^T \rangle$ is diagonal. If we use the eigenvectors of the covariance matrix $\langle RR^T \rangle$ as the columns of the matrix X in the APT equation $R = X b + u$ above, we will find via elementary linear algebra that $\langle bb^T \rangle$ is indeed diagonal; and furthermore, the eigenvalues of $\langle RR^T \rangle$ are none other than the variances of the factor returns b. But of course, there is no point to use factor analysis if the number of factors is the same as the number of stocks—typically, we can just pick the eigenvectors with the top few eigenvalues to form the matrix X. The number of eigenvectors to pick is a parameter that you can adjust to optimize your trading model.

In the following MATLAB program (epchan.com/book/example7_4.m), I illustrate a possible trading strategy applying PCA to S&P 600 small-cap stocks. It is a strategy based on the assumption that factor returns have momentum: They remain constant from the current time period to the next. Hence, we can buy the stocks with the highest expected returns based on these factors, and short the ones with the lowest expected returns. You will find that the average return of this strategy is negative, indicating that this assumption may be quite inaccurate, or that specific returns are too large for this strategy to work.

```
clear;

% use lookback days as estimation (training) period
% for determining factor exposures.
lookback=252;numFactors=5; % Use only 5 factors
% for trading strategy, long stocks with topN expected
1-day returns.
topN=50;
% test on SP600 smallcap stocks. (This MATLAB binary
% input file contains tday, stocks, op, hi, lo, cl
% arrays.)
load('IJR_20080114');
mycls=fillMissingData(cl);

positionsTable=zeros(size(cl));

% note the rows of dailyret are the observations at
% different time periods
dailyret= (mycls-lag1(mycls))/lag1(mycls);
for t=lookback+1:length(tday)

    % here the columns of R are the different
    % observations.
 R=dailyret(t-lookback+1:t,:)';
    % avoid any stocks with missing returns
hasData=find(all(isfinite(R), 2));
    R=R(hasData,:);

    avgR=smartmean(R, 2);
    % subtract mean from returns
 R=R-repmat(avgR, [1 size(R, 2)]);
    % compute covariance matrix, with observations in
    % rows.
 covR=smartcov(R');
    % X is the factor exposures matrix, B the
```

```
    % variances of factor returns.  Use the
    % eigenvectors of covR as column vectors
    % for X.
    [X, B]=eig(covR);
    % Retain only numFactors
  X(:, 1:size(X, 2)-numFactors)=[];
    % b are the factor returns for time period t-1
    % to t.
  results=ols(R(:, end), X);    b=results.beta;

    % Rexp is the expected return for next period
    % assuming factor returns remain constant.
  Rexp=avgR+X*b;
    [foo idxSort]=sort(Rexp, 'ascend');

    % short topN stocks with lowest expected returns
    positionsTable(t, hasData(idxSort(1:topN)))=-1;
    % buy topN stocks with highest expected returns
    positionsTable(t, ..
    hasData(idxSort(end-topN+1:end)))=1;
end

% compute daily returns of trading strategy
ret=..
smartsum(backshift(1, positionsTable).*dailyret, 2);
% compute annualized average return of
% trading strategy
avgret=smartmean(ret)*252;% A very poor return!
% avgret =
%
%    -1.8099
```

This program made use of a function smartcov, which computes a co-variance matrix based on the daily return vectors of many stocks. In contrast to the MATLAB built-in function cov, it ignores days with no returns (i.e., those with NaN values.)

```
function y = smartcov(x)
% Covariance n of finite elements.
% Rows of observations, columns of variables
%    Normalizes by N, not N-1

y=NaN(size(x, 2), size(x, 2));
xc=NaN(size(x));

goodstk=find(~all(isnan(x), 1));
```

```
xc(:, goodstk)=..
x(:, goodstk)-repmat(smartmean(x(:, goodstk),1), ..
[size(x, 1) 1]);  % Remove mean

for m=1:length(goodstk)
    for n=m:length(goodstk)
        y(goodstk(m), goodstk(n))=..
            smartmean(xc(:, goodstk(m)).*..
            xc(:, goodstk(n)));
        y(goodstk(n), goodstk(m))=..
            y(goodstk(m), goodstk(n));
    end
end
```

How good are the performances of factor models in real trading? Naturally, it mostly depends on which factor model we are looking at. But one can make a general observation that factor models that are dominated by fundamental and macroeconomic factors have one major drawback—they depend on the fact that investors persist in using the same metric to value companies. This is just another way of saying that the factor returns must have momentum for factor models to work.

For example, even though the value (book-to-price ratio) factor returns are usually positive, there are periods of time when investors prefer growth stocks such as during the Internet bubble in the late 1990s, and in August and December of 2007. As *The Economist* noted, one reason growth stocks were back in favor in 2007 is the simple fact that their price premium over value stocks has narrowed significantly (*Economist*, 2007b). Another reason is that as the U.S. economy slowed, investors increasingly opted for companies that still managed to generate increasing earnings instead of those that were hurt by the recessionary economy.

Therefore, it is not uncommon for factor models to experience steep drawdown during the times when investors' valuation method shifts, even if only for a short duration. But then, this problem is common to practically any trading model that holds stocks overnight.

WHAT IS YOUR EXIT STRATEGY?

While entry signals are very specific to each trading strategy, there isn't usually much variety in the way exit signals are generated. They are based on one of these:

- A fixed holding period
- A target price or profit cap
- The latest entry signals
- A stop price

A fixed holding period is the default exit strategy for any trading strategy, whether it is a momentum model, a reversal model, or some kind of seasonal trading strategy, which can be either momentum or reversal based. (More on this later.) I said before that one of the ways momentum is generated is the slow diffusion of information. In this case, the process has a finite lifetime. The average value of this finite lifetime determines the optimal holding period, which can usually be discovered in a backtest.

One word of caution on determining the optimal holding period of a momentum model: As I said before, this optimal period typically decreases due to the increasing speed of the diffusion of information and the increasing number of traders who catch on to this trading opportunity. Hence, a momentum model that has worked well with a holding period equal to a week in the backtest period may work only with a one-day holding period now. Worse, the whole strategy may become unprofitable a year into the future. Also, using a backtest of the trading strategy to determine holding period can be fraught with data-snooping bias, since the number of historical trades may be limited. Unfortunately, for a momentum strategy where the trades are triggered by news or events, there are no other alternatives. For a mean-reverting strategy, however, there is a more statistically robust way to determine the optimal holding period that does not depend on the limited number of actual trades.

The mean reversion of a time series can be modeled by an equation called the Ornstein-Uhlenbeck formula (Unlenbeck, 1930). Let's say we denote the mean-reverting spread (long market value minus short market value) of a pair of stocks as *z(t)*. Then we can write

$$dz(t) = -\theta(z(t) - \mu)dt + dW$$

where μ is the mean value of the prices over time, and *dW* is simply some random Gaussian noise. Given a time series of the daily spread values, we can easily find θ (and μ) by performing a linear regression fit of the daily change in the spread *dz* against the spread itself. Mathematicians tell us that the average value of *z(t)* follows an exponential decay to its mean μ, and the half-life of this exponential decay is equal to *ln(2)/θ*, which is the expected time it takes for the spread to revert to half its initial deviation from the mean. This half-life can be used to determine the optimal holding period for a mean-reverting position. Since we can make use of the entire time series to find the best estimate of θ, and not just on the days where a trade was triggered, the estimate for the half-life is much more robust than can be obtained directly from a trading model. In Example 7.5, I demonstrate this method of estimating the half-life of mean reversion using our favorite spread between GLD and GDX.

Example 7.5: Calculation of the Half-Life of a Mean-Reverting Time Series

We can use the mean-reverting spread between GLD and GDX in Example 7.2 to illustrate the calculation of the half-life of its mean reversion. The MATLAB code is available at epchan.com/book/example7_5.m. (The first part of the program is the same as example7_2.m.)

```
% === Insert example7_2.m in the beginning here ===

prevz=backshift(1, z); % z at a previous time-step
dz=z-prevz;
dz(1)=[];
prevz(1)=[];
% assumes dz=theta*(z-mean(z))dt+w,
% where w is error term
results=ols(dz, prevz-mean(prevz));theta=results.beta;

halflife=-log(2)/theta
```

```
% halflife =
%
%      10.0037
```

The program finds that the half-life for mean reversion of the GLD-GDX is about 10 days, which is approximately how long you should expect to hold this spread before it becomes profitable.

If you believe that your security is mean reverting, then you also have a ready-made target price—the mean value of the historical prices of the security, or μ in the Ornstein-Uhlenbeck formula. This target price can be used together with the half-life as exit signals (exit when either criterion is met).

Target prices can also be used in the case of momentum models if you have a fundamental valuation model of a company. But as fundamental valuation is at best an inexact science, target prices are not as easily justified in momentum models as in mean-reverting models. If it were that easy to profit using target prices based on fundamental valuation, all investors have to do is to check out stock analysts' reports every day to make their investment decisions.

Suppose you are running a trading model, and you entered into a position based on its signal. Some time later, you run this model again. If you find that the sign of this latest signal is opposite to your original position (e.g., the latest signal is "buy" when you have an existing short position), then you have two choices. Either you simply use the latest signal to exit the existing position and become flat or you can exit the existing position and then enter into an opposite position. Either way, you have used a new, more recent entry signal as an exit signal for your existing position. This is a common way to generate exit signals when a trading model can be run in shorter intervals than the optimal holding period.

Notice that this strategy of exiting a position based on running an entry model also tells us whether a stop-loss strategy is recommended. In a momentum model, when a more recent entry signal is opposite to an existing position, it means that the direction of momentum has changed, and thus a loss (or more precisely, a drawdown) in your position has been incurred. Exiting this position now is almost akin to a stop loss. However, rather than imposing an arbitrary stop-loss price and thus introducing an extra adjustable parameter, which invites data-snooping bias, exiting based on the most recent entry signal is clearly justified based on the rationale for the momentum model.

Consider a parallel situation when we are running a reversal model. If an existing position has incurred a loss, running the reversal model again will simply generate a new signal with the same sign. Thus, a reversal model for entry signals will never recommend a stop loss. (On the contrary, it can recommend a target price or profit cap when the reversal has gone so far as to hit the opposite entry threshold.) And, indeed, it is much more reasonable to exit a position recommended by a mean-reversal model based on holding period or profit cap than stop loss, as a stop loss in this case often means you are exiting at the worst possible time. (The only exception is when you believe that you have suddenly entered into a momentum regime because of recent news.)

SEASONAL TRADING STRATEGIES

This type of trading strategy is also called the *calendar effect*. Generally, these strategies recommend that you buy or sell certain securities at a fixed date of every year, and close the position at another fixed date. These strategies have been applied to both equity and commodity futures markets. However, from my own experience, much of the seasonality in equity markets has weakened or even disappeared in recent years, perhaps due to the widespread knowledge of this trading opportunity, whereas some seasonal trades in commodity futures are still profitable.

The most famous seasonal trade in equities is called the *January effect*. There are actually many versions of this trade. One version states that small-cap stocks that had the worst returns in the previous calendar year will have higher returns in January than small-cap stocks that had the best returns (Singal, 2006). The rationale for this is that investors like to sell their losers in December to benefit from tax losses, which creates additional downward pressure on their prices. When this pressure disappeared in January, the prices recovered somewhat. This strategy did not work in 2006–07, but worked wonderfully in January 2008, which was a spectacular month for mean-reversal strategies. (That January was the one that saw a major trading scandal at Société Générale, which indirectly may have caused the Federal Reserve to have an emergency 75-basis-point rate cut before the market opened. The turmoil slaughtered many momentum strategies, but mean-reverting strategies benefited greatly from the initial severe downturn and then dramatic rescue by the Fed.) The codes for backtesting this January effect strategy is given in Example 7.6.

Example 7.6: Backtesting the January Effect

Here is the MATLAB code to compute the returns of a strategy applied to S&P 600 small-cap stocks based on the January effect. (The source codes can be found at epchan.com/book/example7_6.m, and the input data is also available there.)

```
clear;

load('IJR_20080131');
onewaytcost=0.0005; % 5bp one way transaction cost

years=..
year(cellstr(datestr(datenum(cellstr(..
num2str(tday)), 'yyyymmdd')))) ;
months=..
month(cellstr(datestr(datenum(cellstr(..
num2str(tday)), 'yyyymmdd')))) ;

nextdayyear=fwdshift(1, years);
nextdaymonth=fwdshift(1, months);

lastdayofDec=find(months==12 & nextdaymonth==1);
lastdayofJan=find(months==1 & nextdaymonth==2);

% lastdayofDec starts in 2004,
% so remove 2004 from lastdayofJan
lastdayofJan(1)=[];% Ensure each lastdayofJan date
after each
% lastdayofDec date
```

```
assert(all(tday(lastdayofJan) > tday(lastdayofDec)));
eoy=find(years~=nextdayyear); % End Of Year indices

eoy(end)=[]; % last index is not End of Year

% Ensure eoy dates match lastdayofDec dates
assert(all(tday(eoy)==tday(lastdayofDec)));
annret=..
(cl(eoy(2:end),:)-cl(eoy(1:end-1),:))./..
cl(eoy(1:end-1),:); % annual returns
janret=..
(cl(lastdayofJan(2:end),:)-
cl(lastdayofDec(2:end),:))./cl(lastdayofDec(2:end),:);
% January returns

for y=1:size(annret, 1)
    % pick those stocks with valid annual returns
    hasData=..
    find(isfinite(annret(y,:)));
    % sort stocks based on prior year's returns
    [foo sortidx]=sort(annret(y, hasData), 'ascend');
    % buy stocks with lowest decile of returns,
    % and vice versa for highest decile
 topN=round(length(hasData)/10);
    % portfolio returns
  portRet=..
  (smartmean(janret(y, hasData(sortidx(1:topN)))))-..
  smartmean(janret(y, hasData(..
  sortidx(end-topN+1:end)))))/2-2*onewaytcost;
    fprintf(1,'Last holding date %i: Portfolio
 return=%7.4f\n', tday(lastdayofDec(y+1)), portRet);
end
% These should be the output
% Last holding date 20051230: Portfolio return=-0.0244
% Last holding date 20061229: Portfolio return=-0.0068
% Last holding date 20071231: Portfolio return= 0.0881
```

This program uses a number of utility programs. The first one is the assert function, which is very useful for ensuring the program is working as expected.

```
function assert(pred, str)
% ASSERT Raise an error if the predicate is not true.
% assert(pred, string)

if nargin<2, str = ''; end
```

```
if ~pred
  s = sprintf('assertion violated: %s', str);
  error(s);
end
```

The second one is the fwdshift function, which works in the opposite way
to the lag1 function: It shifts the time series one step forward.

```
function y=fwdshift(day,x)
assert(day>=0);

y=[x(day+1:end,:,:); ..
NaN*ones(day,size(x,2), size(x, 3))];
```

Another seasonal strategy in equities was proposed more
recently (Heston and Sadka, 2007; available at lcb1.uoregon.
edu/rcg/seminars/seasonal072604.pdf). This strategy is very simple:
each month, buy a number of stocks that performed the best in the
same month a year earlier, and short the same number of stocks
that performed poorest in that month a year earlier. The average
annual return before 2002 was more than 13 percent before transaction costs. However, I have found that this effect has disappeared
since then, as you can check for yourself in Example 7.7. (See
the readers' comments to my blog post epchan.blogspot.com/2007/
11/seasonal-trades-in-stocks.html.)

Example 7.7: Backtesting a Year-on-Year Seasonal Trending Strategy

Here is the MATLAB code for the year-on-year seasonal trending strategy
I quoted earlier. (The source code can be downloaded from epchan.com/
book/example7_7.m. The data is also available at that site.) Note that the
data contains survivorship bias, as it is based on the S&P 500 index on
November 23, 2007.

```
clear;

load('SPX_20071123', 'tday', 'stocks', 'cl');
```

```
% find the indices of the days that are at month ends.
monthEnds=find(isLastTradingDayOfMonth(tday));
monthlyRet=..
(cl(monthEnds,:)-lag1(cl(monthEnds,:)))./..
lag1(cl(monthEnds,:));

mycl=fillMissingData(cl);

% sort stocks by monthly returns in ascending order
 [monthlyRetSorted sortIndex]=sort(monthlyRet, 2);
% these are the sorted monthly returns of the
  previous year
prevYearMonthlyRetSorted=backshift(12,
monthlyRetSorted);% the sort index of the
previous year
prevYearSortIndex=backshift(12, sortIndex);
positions=zeros(size(monthlyRet));

for m=13:size(monthlyRet, 1)
    hasReturns=. . .
    isfinite(prevYearMonthlyRetSorted(m,:)) & ..
    isfinite(cl(monthEnds(m-1),:));
    mySortIndex=prevYearSortIndex(m, hasReturns);

    % take top decile of stocks as longs,
    % bottom decile as shorts
 topN=floor(length(mySortIndex)/10);
    positions(m-1, mySortIndex(1:topN))=-1;
    positions(m-1, ..
      mySortIndex(end-topN+1:end))=1;
end

ret=smartsum(lag1(positions).*monthlyRet, 2);

avgannret=12*smartmean(ret);
sharpe=sqrt(12)*smartmean(ret)/smartstd(ret);

fprintf(1, ..
 'Avg ann return=%7.4f Sharpe ratio=%7.4f\n', ..
 avgannret, sharpe);
% Output should be
% Avg ann return=-0.9167 Sharpe ratio=-0.1055
```

This program contains a few utility functions. The first one is LastTrading-DayOfMonth, which returns a logical array of 1s and 0s, indicating whether a month in a trading-date array is the last trading day of a month.

```
function isLastTradingDayOfMonth=..
 isLastTradingDayOfMonth(tday)
% isLastTradingDayOfMonth=
% isLastTradingDayOfMonth(tday) returns a logical
% array. True if tday(t) is last trading day of month.

tdayStr=datestr(datenum(num2str(tday), 'yyyymmdd'));

todayMonth=month(tdayStr);

tmrMonth=fwdshift(1, todayMonth); % tomorrow's month

isLastTradingDayOfMonth=false(size(tday));

isLastTradingDayOfMonth(todayMonth~=tmrMonth & ..
 isfinite(todayMonth) & isfinite(tmrMonth))=true;
```

Another is the backshift function, which is like the lag1 function except that one can shift any arbitrary number of periods instead of just 1.

```
function y=backshift(day,x)
% y=backshift(day,x)
assert(day>=0);
y=[NaN(day,size(x,2), size(x, 3));x(1:end-day,:,:)];
```

You can try the most recent five years instead of the entire data period, and you will find that the average returns are even worse.

In contrast to equity seasonal strategies, commodity futures' seasonal strategies are alive and well. That is perhaps because seasonal demand for certain commodities is driven by "real" economic needs rather than speculations.

One of the most intuitive commodity seasonal trades is the gasoline future trade: Simply buy the gasoline future contract that expires in May near the middle of April, and sell it by the end of April. This trade has been profitable for the last 11 years, as of this writing in April 2008. (See the sidebar for details.) It appears that one can always depend on approaching summer driving seasons in North America to drive up gasoline futures prices in the spring.

A SEASONAL TRADE IN GASOLINE FUTURES

Whenever the summer driving season comes up, it should not surprise us that gasoline futures prices will be rising seasonally. The only question for the trader is: which month contract to buy, and to hold for what period? After scanning the literature, the best trade I have found so far is one where we buy 1 contract of RB (the unleaded gasoline futures trading on the New York Mercantile Exchange [NYMEX]) at the close of April 13 (or the following trading day if it is a holiday), and sell it at the close of April 25 (or the previous trading day if it is a holiday). Historically, we would have realized a profit every year since 1995. Here is the annual profit and loss (P&L) and maximum drawdown (measured from day 1, the entry point) experienced by this position (the 2007–08 numbers are from actual trading):

Year	P&L in $	Maximum Drawdown in $
1995	1,037	0
1996	1,638	−2,226
1997	227	−664
1998	118	0
1999	197	−588
2000	735	−315
2001	1,562	0
2002	315	0
2003	1,449	−38
2004	361	−907
2005	6,985	−25
2006	890	0
2007*	2,286	−9,816
2008*	4,741	0

*Actual trading result expressed as 2 × QU.

For those who desire less risk, you can buy the mini gasoline futures QU at NYMEX which trade at half the size of RB, though it is illiquid.

(This research has been inspired by the monthly seasonal trades published by Paul Kavanaugh at PFGBest.com. You can read up on this and other seasonal futures patterns in Fielden, 2005, or Toepke, 2004.)

Besides demand for gasoline, natural gas demand also goes up as summer approaches due to increasing demand from power generators to provide electricity for air conditioning. Hence, another commodity seasonal trade that has been profitable for 13 consecutive

years as of this writing is the natural gas trade: Buy the natural gas
future contract that expires in June near the end of February, and
sell it by the middle of April. (Again, see sidebar for details.)

Summer season is also when natural gas demand goes up due to the increasing
demand from power generators to provide electricity for air conditioning. This
suggests a seasonal trade in natural gas where we long a June contract of NYMEX
natural gas futures (Symbol: NG) at the close of February 25 (or the following
trading day if it is a holiday), and exit this position on April 15 (or the previous
trading day if it is a holiday). This trade has been profitable for 14 consecutive
years at of this writing. Here is the annual P&L and maximum drawdown of this
trade, both in backtest and in actual trading:

Year	P&L in $	Maximum Drawdown in $
1995	1,970	0
1996	3,090	−630
1997	450	−430
1998	2,150	−1,420
1999	4,340	−370
2000	4,360	0
2001	2,730	−1,650
2002	9,860	0
2003	2,000	−5,550
2004	5,430	0
2005	2,380	−230
2006	2,250	−1,750
2007	800	−7,470
2008*	10,137	−1,604

*Actual trading results expressed as 4 × QG.

Natural gas futures are notoriously volatile, and we have seen big trading
losses for hedge funds (e.g., Amaranth Advisors, loss = $6 billion) and major
banks (e.g., Bank of Montreal, loss = $450 million). Therefore, one should be
cautious if one wants to try out this trade—perhaps at reduced capital using the
mini QG futures at half the size of the full NG contract.

*This article originally appeared in my subscription area epchan.com/subscription, and is
updated with the latest numbers. You can access that area using "sharperatio" as username
and password.

Commodity futures seasonal trades do suffer from one draw-back despite their consistent profitability: they typically occur only once a year; therefore, it is hard to tell whether the backtest performance is a result of data-snooping bias. As usual, one way to alleviate this problem is to try somewhat different entry and exit dates to see if the profitability holds up. In addition, one should consider only those trades where the seasonality makes some economic sense. The gasoline and natural gas trades amply satisfy these criteria.

HIGH-FREQUENCY TRADING STRATEGIES

In general, if a high Sharpe ratio is the goal of your trading strategy (as it should be, given what I said in Chapter 6), then you should be trading at high frequencies, rather than holding stocks overnight.

What are high-frequency trading strategies, and why do they have superior Sharpe ratios? Many experts in high-frequency trading would not regard any strategy that holds positions for more than a few seconds as high frequency, but here I would take a more pedestrian approach and include any strategy that does not hold a position overnight. Many of the early high-frequency strategies were applied to the foreign exchange market, and then later on to the futures market, because of their abundance of liquidity. In the last six or seven years, however, with the increasing liquidity in the equity market, the availability of historical tick database for stocks, and mushrooming computing power, this type of strategies has become widespread for stock trading as well.

The reason why these strategies have Sharpe ratio is simple: Based on the "law of large numbers," the more bets you can place, the smaller the percent deviation from the mean return you will experience. With high-frequency trading, one can potentially place hundreds if not thousands of bets all in one day. Therefore, provided the strategy is sound and generates positive mean return, you can expect the day-to-day deviation from this return to be minimal. With this high Sharpe ratio, one can increase the leverage to a much higher level than longer-term strategies can, and this high leverage in turn boosts the return-on-equity of the strategy to often stratospheric levels.

Of course, the law of large numbers does not explain why a particular high-frequency strategy has positive mean return in the first place. In fact, it is impossible to explain in general why high-frequency strategies are often profitable, as there are as many such strategies as there are fund managers. Some of them are mean reverting, while others are trend following. Some are market-neutral pair traders, while others are long-only directional traders. In general, though, these strategies aim to exploit tiny inefficiencies in the market or to provide temporary liquidity needs for a small fee. Unlike betting on macroeconomic trends or company fundamentals where the market environment can experience upheavals during the lifetime of a trade, such inefficiencies and need for liquidity persist day to day, allowing consistent daily profits to be made. Furthermore, high-frequency strategies typically trade securities in modest sizes. Without large positions to unwind, risk management for high-frequency portfolios is fairly easy: "Deleveraging" can be done very quickly in the face of losses, and certainly one can stop trading and be completely in cash when the going gets truly rough. The worst that can happen as these strategies become more popular is a slow death as a result of gradually diminishing returns. Sudden drastic losses are not likely, nor are contagious losses across multiple accounts.

Though successful high-frequency strategies have such numerous merits, it is not easy to backtest such strategies when the average holding period decreases to minutes or even seconds. Transaction costs are of paramount importance in testing such strategies. Without incorporating transactions, the simplest strategies may seem to work at high frequencies. As a consequence, just having high-frequency data with last prices is not sufficient—data with bid, ask, and last quotes is needed to find out the profitability of executing on the bid versus the ask. Sometimes, we may even need historical order book information for backtesting. Quite often, the only true test for such strategies is to run it in real-time unless one has an extremely sophisticated simulator.

Backtesting is only a small part of the game in high-frequency trading. High-speed execution may account for a large part of the actual profits or losses. Professional high-frequency trading firms have been writing their strategies in C instead of other, more user-friendly languages, and locating their servers next to the exchange or a major Internet backbone to reduce the microsecond delays. So even though the Sharpe ratio is appealing and the returns astronomical, truly high-frequency trading is not by any means easy for an independent trader to achieve in the beginning. But there is no reason not to work toward this goal gradually as expertise and resources accrue.

IS IT BETTER TO HAVE A HIGH-LEVERAGE VERSUS A HIGH-BETA PORTFOLIO?

In Chapter 6, I discussed the optimal leverage to apply to a portfolio based on the Kelly formula. In the section on factor models earlier in this chapter, I discussed the Fama-French Three-Factor model, which suggests that return of a portfolio (or a stock) is proportional to its beta (if we hold the market capitalization and book value of its stocks fixed). In other words, you can increase return on a portfolio by either increasing its leverage or increasing its beta (by selecting high-beta stocks.) Both ways seem commonsensical. In fact, it is clear that given a low-beta portfolio and a high-beta portfolio, it is easy to apply a higher leverage on the low-beta portfolio so as to increase its beta to match that of the high-beta portfolio. And assuming that the stocks of two portfolios have the same average market capitalizations and book values, the average returns of the two will also be the same (ignoring specific returns, which will decrease in importance as long as we increase the number stocks in the portfolios), according to the Fama-French model. So should we be indifferent to which portfolio to own?

The answer is no. Recall in Chapter 6 that the long-term compounded growth rate of a portfolio, if we use the Kelly leverage, is proportional to the Sharpe ratio squared, and not to the average return. So if the two hypothetical portfolios have the same average return, then we would prefer the one that has the smaller risk or standard deviation. Empirical studies have found that a portfolio that consists of low-beta stocks generally has lower risk and thus a higher Sharpe ratio.

For example, in a paper titled "Risk Parity Portfolios" (not publicly distributed), Dr. Edward Qian at PanAgora Asset Management argued that a typical 60–40 asset allocation between stocks and bonds is not optimal because it is overweighted with risky assets (stocks in this case). Instead, to achieve a higher Sharpe ratio while maintaining the same risk level as the 60–40 portfolio, Dr. Qian recommended a 23–77 allocation while leveraging the entire portfolio by 1.8.

Somehow, the market is chronically underpricing high-beta stocks. Hence, given a choice between a portfolio of high-beta stocks and a portfolio of low-beta stocks, we should prefer the low-beta one, which we can then leverage up to achieve the maximum compounded growth rate.

There is one usual caveat, however. All this is based on the Gaussian assumption of return distributions. (See discussions in Chapter 6 on this issue.) Since the actual returns distributions have fat tails, one should be quite wary of using too much leverage on normally low-beta stocks.

SUMMARY

This book has been largely about a particular type of quantitative trading called *statistical arbitrage* in the investment industry. Despite this fancy name, statistical arbitrage is actually far simpler than trading derivatives (e.g., options) or fixed-income instruments, both conceptually and mathematically. I have described a large part of the statistical arbitrageur's standard arsenal: mean reversion and momentum, regime switching, stationarity and cointegration, arbitrage pricing theory or factor model, seasonal trading models, and, finally, high-frequency trading.

Some of the important points to note can be summarized here:

- Mean-reverting regimes are more prevalent than trending regimes.
- There are some tricky data issues involved with backtesting mean-reversion strategies: Outlier quotes and survivorship bias are among them.
- Trending regimes are usually triggered by the diffusion of new information, the execution of a large institutional order, or "herding" behavior.
- Competition between traders tends to reduce the number of mean-reverting trading opportunities.
- Competition between traders tends to reduce the optimal holding period of a momentum trade.
- Regime switching can sometimes be detected using a data-miningx approach with numerous input features.
- A stationary price series is ideal for a mean-reversion trade.
- Two or more nonstationary price series can be combined to form a stationary one if they are "cointegrating."
- Cointegration and correlation are different things: Cointegration is about the long-term behavior of the *prices* of two or more stocks, while correlation is about the short-term behavior of their *returns*.
- Factor models, or arbitrage pricing theory, are commonly used for modeling how fundamental factors affect stock returns linearly.
- One of the most well-known factor models is the Fama-French Three-Factor model, which postulates that stock returns are proportional to their beta and book-to-price ratio, and negatively to their market capitalizations.
- Factor models typically have a relatively long holding period and long drawdowns due to regime switches.
- Exit signals should be created differently for mean-reversion versus momentum strategies.
- Estimation of the optimal holding period of a mean-reverting strategy can be quite robust, due to the Ornstein-Uhlenbeck formula.

- Estimation of the optimal holding period of a momentum strategy can be error prone due to the small number of signals.
- Stop loss can be suitable for momentum strategies but not reversal strategies.
- Seasonal trading strategies for stocks (i.e., calendar effect) have become unprofitable in recent years.
- Seasonal trading strategies for commodity futures continue to be profitable.
- High-frequency trading strategies rely on the "law of large numbers" for their high Sharpe ratios.
- High-frequency trading strategies typically generate the highest long-term compounded growth due to their high Sharpe ratios.
- High-frequency trading strategies are very difficult to backtest and very technology reliant for their execution.
- Holding a highly leveraged portfolio of low-beta stocks should generate higher long-term compounded growth than holding unleveraged portfolio of high-beta stocks.

Most statistical arbitrage trading strategies are some combination of these effects or models: Whether they are profitable or not is more of an issue of where and when to apply them than whether they are theoretically correct or not.

CHAPTER 8

Conclusion

Can Independent Traders Succeed?

Quantitative trading gained notoriety in the summer of 2007 when some enormous hedge funds run by some of the most reputable money managers rung up losses measured in billions in just a few days (though some had recovered by the end of the month). They brought back bad memories of other notorious hedge fund debacles such as that of Long-Term Capital Management and Amaranth Advisors (both referenced in Chapter 6), except that this time it was not just one trader or one firm, but losses at multiple funds over a short period of time.

And yet, ever since I began my career in the institutional quantitative trading business, I have spoken to many small, independent traders, working in shabby offices or their spare bedrooms, who gain small but steady and growing profits year-in and year-out, quite unlike the stereotypical reckless day traders of the popular imagination. In fact, many independent traders that I know of have not only survived the periods when big funds lost billions, but actually thrived in those times. This has been the central mystery of trading to me for many years: how does an independent trader with insignificant equity and minimal infrastructure trade with high Sharpe ratio while firms with all-star teams fail spectacularly?

At the beginning of 2006, I left the institutional money management business and struck out on my own to experience this first-hand. I figured that if I could not trade profitably when I was free of all institutional constraints and politics, then either trading is a hoax or I am just not cut out to be a trader. Either way, I promised myself that in such an event I would quit trading forever. Fortunately, I survived. Along the way, I also found the key to that central mystery to which I alluded earlier.

The key, it turns out, is *capacity*, a concept I introduced at the end of Chapter 2. (To recap: Capacity is the amount of equity a strategy can generate good returns on.) It is far, far easier to generate a high Sharpe ratio trading a $100,000 account than a $100 million account. There are many simple and profitable strategies that can work at the low capacity end that would be totally unsuitable to hedge funds. This is the niche for independent traders like us.

Let me elaborate on this capacity issue. Most profitable strategies that have low capacities are acting as market makers: providing short-term liquidity when it is needed and taking quick profits when the liquidity need disappears. If, however, you have billions of dollars to manage, you now become the party in need of liquidity, and you have to pay for it. To minimize the cost of this liquidity demand, you necessarily have to hold your positions over long periods of time. When you hold for long periods, your portfolio will be subject to macroeconomic changes (i.e., regime shifts) that can cause great damage to your portfolio. Though you may still be profitable in the long run if your models are sound, you cannot avoid the occasional sharp drawdowns that attract newspaper headlines.

Other disadvantages beset large-capacity strategies favored by large institutions. The intense competition among hedge funds means the strategies become less profitable. The lowered returns in turn pressure the fund manager to overleverage. To beat out the competition, traders need to resort to more and more complicated models, which in turn invite data-snooping bias. But despite the increasing complexity of the models, the fundamental market inefficiency that they are trying to exploit may remain the same, and thus their portfolios may still end up holding very similar positions. We discussed this phenomenon in Chapter 6. When market environment changes, a stampede out of similar losing positions can (and did) cause a complete meltdown of the market.

Another reason that independent traders can often succeed when large funds fail is the myriad constraints imposed by management in an institutional setting. For example, as a trader in a quantitative fund, you may be prohibited from trading a long-only strategy, but long-only strategies are often easier to find, simpler, more profitable, and if traded in small sizes, no more risky than market-neutral strategies. Or you may be prohibited from trading futures. You may be required to be not only market neutral but also sector neutral. You may be asked to find a momentum strategy when you know that a mean-reverting strategy would work. And on and on. Many of these constraints are imposed for risk management reasons, but many others may be just whims, quirks, and prejudices of the management. As every student of mathematical optimization knows, any constraint imposed on an optimization problem decreases the optimal objective value. Similarly, every institutional constraint imposed on a trading strategy tends to decrease its returns, if not its Sharpe ratio as well. Finally, some senior managers who oversee frontline portfolio managers of quantitative funds are actually not well versed in quantitative techniques, and they tend to make decisions based on anything but quantitative theories.

When your strategy shows initial profits, these managers may impose enormous pressure for you to scale up quickly, and when your strategy starts to lose, they may force you to liquidate the portfolios and abandon the strategy immediately. None of these interferences in the quantitative investment process is mathematically optimal.

Besides, such managers often have a mercurial temper, which seldom mixes well with quantitative investment management. When loss of money occurs, rationality is often the first victim.

As an independent trader, you are free from such constraints and interferences, and as long as you are emotionally capable to adhere to the discipline of quantitative trading, your trading environment may actually be closer to the optimal than that of a large fund.

Actually, there is one more reason why it is easier for hedge funds to blow up than for individual traders trading their own accounts to do so. When one is trading other people's money, one's upside is almost unlimited, while the downside is simply to get fired. Hence, despite the pro forma adherence to stringent institutional risk management procedures and constraints, one is fundamentally driven to trade strategies that are more risky in an institutional setting, as long as you can sneak past the risk manager. But Mr. Jérôme Kerviel at Société Générale has shown us that this is not at all difficult!

L'Affaire Société Générale cost the bank $7.1 billion and may have indirectly led to an emergency Fed rate cut in the United States. The bank's internal controls failed to discover the rogue trades for three years because Mr. Kerviel has worked in the back office and has gained great familiarity with ways to evade the control procedures (Clark, 2008).

In fact, Mr. Kerviel's deceptive technique is by no means original. When I was working at a large investment bank, there was a pair of proprietary traders who traded quantitatively. They were enclosed in a glass bubble at a corner of the vast trading floor, either because they could not be bothered by the hustle and bustle of the nonquantitative traders, or they had to keep their trade secrets, well, secret. As far as I could tell, neither of them ever talked to anyone. Nor, it seemed, did they ever speak to each other.

One day, one of the traders disappeared, never to return. Shortly thereafter, hordes of auditors were searching through his files and computers. It turned out that, just like Mr. Kerviel, this trader had worked in the information technology (IT) department and was quite computer savvy. He managed to manufacture many millions of false profits without anyone's questioning him until, one day, a computer crash somehow stopped his rogue program in its track and exposed his activities. Rumor had it that he disappeared to India and has been enjoying the high life ever since.

So there you have it. I hope I have made a convincing case that independent traders can gain an edge over institutional traders, if trading is conducted with discipline and care. Of course, the side benefits of being independent are numerous, and they begin with freedom. Personally, I am much happier with my work now than I have ever been in my career, despite the inevitable gut-wrenching drawdowns from time to time.

NEXT STEPS

So let's say you have found a few good, simple strategies and are happily trading in your spare bedroom. Where do you go from here? How do you *grow*?

Actually, I discussed growth in Chapter 6, but in a limited sense. Using the Kelly formula, you can indeed achieve exponential growth of your equity, but only up to the total capacity of your strategies. After that, the source of growth has to come from increasing the number of strategies. You can, for example, look for strategies that trade at higher frequencies than the ones you currently have. To do that, you have to invest and upgrade your technological infrastructure, and purchase expensive high-frequency historical data. Or, conversely, you can look for strategies that hold longer periods. Despite their typically lower Sharpe ratios, they do enormously improve your capacity. For many of these strategies, you probably have to invest in expensive historical fundamental data for your backtest. If you are an equity trader, you can branch out into futures or currencies, which typically have higher capacities than equity models. If you run out of ideas or lack expertise in a new market that you want to enter, you can form collaborations with other like-minded traders, or you can hire consultants to help with the research. If you are running too many strategies to manage manually on your own, you can push your automation further so that there is no need for you to manually intervene in the daily trading unless exceptions or problems occur. Of course, you can also hire a trader to monitor all these strategies for you.

These investments in data, infrastructure, and personnel are all part of reinvesting some of your earnings to further the growth of your trading business, not unlike growing any other type of business. When you have reached a point where your capacity is higher than what the Kelly formula suggests you can prudently utilize, it may be time for you to start taking on investors, who will at the very least defray the costs of your infrastructure, if not provide an incentive fee. Alternatively, you might want to take your strategy (and, more importantly, your track record) to one of the larger hedge funds and ask for a profit-sharing contract.

After the recent major losses at quantitative hedge funds, many people have started to wonder if quantitative trading is viable in the long term. Though the talk of the demise of quantitative strategies appears to be premature at this point, it is still an important question from the perspective of an independent trader. Once you have automated everything and your equity is growing exponentially, can you just sit back, relax, and enjoy your wealth? Unfortunately, experience tells us that strategies do lose their potency over time as more traders catch on to them. It takes ongoing research to supply you with new strategies.

There are always upheavals and major regime changes that may occur once every decade but will nevertheless cause sudden deaths to certain strategies. As with any commercial endeavor, a period of rapid growth will inevitably be followed by the steady if unspectacular returns of a mature business. As long as financial markets demand instant liquidity, however, there will always be a profitable niche for quantitative trading.

A Quick Survey of MATLAB

ATLAB is a general-purpose software package developed by Mathworks, Inc., which is used by many institutional quantitative researchers and traders as their platform for backtesting, particularly those that work in statistical arbitrage. In Chapter 3, I introduced this platform and compared its pros and cons with some other alternatives. Most of the strategy examples in this book are written in MATLAB. Many of those strategies are portfolio-trading strategies involving hundreds of stocks that are very difficult to backtest in Excel. Here, I will provide a quick survey of MATLAB for those traders who are unfamiliar with the language, so they can see if it is worthwhile for them to invest in acquiring and learning to use this platform for their own backtesting.

MATLAB is not only a programming language; it is also an integrated development platform that includes a very user-friendly program editor and debugger. It is an interpreted language, meaning that similar to Visual Basic, but unlike a conventional programming language like C, it does not need to be compiled before it can be run. Yet it is much more flexible and powerful for backtesting than using Excel or Visual Basic because of the large number of built-in functions useful for mathematical computations, and because it is an array-processing language that is specially designed to make computations on arrays (i.e., vectors or matrices) simply and quickly. In particular, many loops that are necessary in C or Visual Basic can be replaced by just one line of code in MATLAB. It also includes extensive text processing facilities such that it is useful as a powerful tool for parsing and analyzing texts (such as web pages). Furthermore, it has a comprehensive graphics library that enables easy plotting of many types of graphs, even animations. (Many of the figures and charts in this book are created using MATLAB.) Finally, MATLAB codes can be compiled into C or C++ executables that can run on computers without the MATLAB platform installed. In fact, there is third-party software that can convert MATLAB code into C source codes, too.

The basic syntax of MATLAB is very similar to Visual Basic or C. For example, we can initialize the elements of an array x like this:

```
x(1)=0.1;
x(2)=0.3;
% 3 elements of an array initialized.
% This is by default a row-vector
x(3)=0.2;
```

Note that we don't need to first "declare" this array, nor do we need to tell MATLAB its expected size beforehand. If you leave out the ";" sign, MATLAB will print out the result of the content of the variable being assigned a value. Any comments can be written after the "%" sign. If you wish, you can initialize a large number of elements en masse to a common value:

```
% assigning the value 0.8 to all elements of a 3-vector y.
This is a row-vector.y=0.8*ones(1, 3)
```

Now if you want to do a vector addition of the two vectors, you can do it the old-fashioned way (just as you would in C), that is, using a loop:

```
for i=1:3
     z(i)=x(i)+y(i) % z is [0.9 1.1 1]
end
```

But the power of MATLAB is that it can handle many array operations in parallel very succinctly, without using loops. (That's why it is called a vector-processing language.) So instead of the loop above, you can just write

```
z=x+y % z is the same [0.9 1.1 1]
```

Even more powerful, you can easily select part of the different arrays and operate on them. What do you think would be the results of the following?

```
w=x([1 3])+z([2 1])
```

x([1 3]) selected the first and third elements of x, so x([1 3]) is just [0.1 0.2]. z([2 1]) selected the second and first elements of y, *in that order*, so z([2 1]) is [1.1 0.9]. So w is [1.2 1.1].

You can delete parts of an array just as easily:

```
x([1 3])=[] % this leaves x as [0.3]
```

To concatenate two arrays is also trivial. To concatenate by rows, use the ";" to separate the arrays:

```
u=[z([1 1]); w]
% u is now
% [0.9000    0.9000;
 % 1.2000    1.1000]
```

To concatenate by columns, omit the ";":

```
v=[z([1 1]) w]
% v is now
% [0.9000    0.9000    1.2000    1.1000]
```

Selection of a subarray can be done not only with arrays containing indices; it can be done with arrays containing logical values as well. For example, here is a logical array:

```
vlogical=v<1.1
% vlogical is [1 1 0 0], where the 0s and 1's
% indicate whether that element is less than 1.1 or
% not.

vlt=v(vlogical) % vlt is [0.9 0.9]
```

In fact, we can select the same subarray with the oft-used short-hand

```
vlt=v(v<1.1) % vlt is the same [0.9 0.9]
```

If, for some reasons, you are interested in the actual indices of the elements of v that have value less than 1.1, you can use the "find" function:

```
idx=find(v<1.1); % idx is [1 2]
```

Naturally, you can use this index array to select the same sub-array as before:

```
vlt=v(idx); % vlt is the again same [0.9 0.9]
```

So far, the array examples are all one-dimensional. But of course, MATLAB can deal with multidimensional arrays as well. Here is a two-dimensional example:

```
x=[1 2 3; 4 5 6; 7 8 9];
% x is
%   1   2   3
%   4   5   6
%   7   8   9
```

You can select the entire row or column of multi-dimensional array by using the ":" symbol. For example,

```
xr1=x(1,:) % xr1 is the first row of x, i.e. xr1 is [1 2 3]

xc2=x(:, 2)% xc2 is the second column of x, i.e. xc2 is
% 2
% 5
% 8
```

Naturally, you can delete an entire row from an array using the same method.

```
x(1,:) =[] % x is now just [4 5 6; 7 8 9]
```

The transpose of a matrix is indicated by a simple "'". So the transpose of x is just x', which is

```
4       7
5       8
6       9
```

Elements of arrays do not have to be numbers. They can be strings, or even arrays themselves. This kind of arrays is called cell array in MATLAB. In the following example, C is just such a cell array:

```
C={[1 2 3]; ['a' 'b' 'c' 'd']}
% C is
% [1 2 3]
  % 'abcd'
```

One of the beauties of MATLAB is that practically all built-in functions can work on all elements of arrays concurrently. For example,

```
log(x) % this gives
     % 1.3863    1.6094    1.7918
     % 1.9459    2.0794    2.1972
```

There are a large number of such built-in functions. Some of the ones I have used are:

```
sum, cumsum, diag, max, min, mean, std, corrcoef,
repmat, reshape, squeeze, sort, sortrow, rand, size,
length, eigs, fix, round, floor, ceil, mod,
factorial, setdiff, union, intersect, ismember,
unique, any, all, eval, eye, ones, strmatch, regexp,
regexprep, plot, hist, bar, scatter, try, catch,
circshift, datestr, datenum, isempty, isfinite,
isnan, islogical, randperm
```

If the built-in functions of the basic MATLAB platform do not meet all your needs, you can always purchase additional toolboxes from MATLAB. Some of the toolboxes useful to quantitative traders are the optimization, partial differential equations (for derivative traders), genetic algorithms, statistics, neural networks, signal processing, wavelet, financial, financial derivatives, GARCH, financial times series, datafeed, and fixed-income toolboxes. If these toolboxes are too costly, or if they still do not meet all your needs, there are also a number of free user-contributed toolboxes available for download from the Internet. I have introduced one of them in this book: the Econometrics toolbox developed by James LeSage (www.spatial-econometrics.com). There are a number of others that I have used before: the Bayes Net toolbox from Kevin Murphy (www.cs.ubc.ca/~murphyk/Software/BNT/bnt.html), or the GARCH toolbox from Kevin Sheppard (www.kevinsheppard. org/research/ucsd_garch/ucsd_garch.aspx). The easy availability of these user-contributed toolboxes and the large community of MATLAB users from whom you can ask for help greatly enhance the usefulness of MATLAB as a computational platform.

You can, of course, write your own functions in MATLAB, too. I have given a number of example functions in this book, all of which can be downloaded from my web site, www.epchan.com/book. In fact, it is very helpful for you to develop your own library of utilities functions that you often use for constructing trading strategies. As this homegrown library grows, your productivity in developing new strategies will increase as well.

Bibliography

Alexander, Carol. 2001. *Market Models: A Guide to Financial Data Analysis*. West Sussex: John Wiley & Sons Ltd.

Chai, Soo, and Joon Lim. 2007. "Economic Turning Point Forecasting Using Neural Network with Weighted Fuzzy Membership Functions." Lecture Notes in Computer Science, Springer.

Clark, Nicola. 2008. "French Bank Says Its Controls Failed for 2 Years." *New York Times*, Febrary 21. Available at: http://www.nytimes.com/2008/02/21/business/worldbusiness/21bank.html?ex=1361336400&en=cf84f3776a877eac&ei=5124&partner=permalink&exprod=permalink.

Cover, Thomas. 1991. "Universal Portfolios." *Mathematical Finance* 1(1): 1–29.

Duhigg, Charles. 2006. "Street Scene; A Smarter Computer to Pick Stock." *New York Times*, November 24.

Economist. 2007a. "Too Much Information." July 12. Available at: www.economist.com/finance/displaystory.cfm?story_id=9482952.

Economist. 2007b. "This Year's Model." December 13. Available at: www.economist.com/finance/displaystory.cfm?story_id=10286619.

Fama, Eugene, and Kenneth French. 1992. "The Cross-Section of Expected Stock Returns." *Journal of Finance* XLVII(2): 427–465.

Fielden, Sandy. 2006. "Seasonal Surprises." *Energy Risk*, September. Available at: www.lim.com/pdfdocs/marketing/marketfocus_sept05.pdf.

Grinold, Richard, and Ronald Kahn. 1999. *Active Portfolio Management*. New York: McGraw-Hill.

Kaufmann, Sylvia, and Martin Scheicher. 1996. "Markov-Regime Switching in Economic Variables: Part I. Modelling, Estimating and Testing. Part II. A Selective Survey." Institute for Advanced Studies Economics Series no. 38.

Klaassen, Franc. 2002. "Improving GARCH Volatility Forecasts with Regime-Switching GARCH." *Empirical Economics* 27(2): 363–394.

Khandani, Amir, and Lo, Andrew. 2007. "What Happened to the Quants in August 2007?" *Preprint*. Available at: web.mit.edu/alo/www/Papers/august07.pdf.

Lux, Hal. 2000. "The Secret World of Jim Simons." *Institutional Investor Magazine*, November 1.

Markoff, John. 2007. "Faster Chips Are Leaving Programmers in Their Dust." *New York Times*, December 17. Available at: www.nytimes.com/2007/12/17/technology/17chip.html?ex=1355634000&en=a81769355deb7953&ei=5124&partner=permalink&exprod=permalink.

Nielsen, Steen, and Jan Overgaard Olesen. 2000. "Regime-Switching Stock Returns and Mean Reversion." Working Paper 11–2000. Department of Economics, Copenhagen Business School.

Oldfield, Richard. 2007. *Simple but Not Easy*. Doddington Publishing.

Poundstone, William. 2005. *Fortune's Formula*. New York: Hill and Wang.

Heston, Steven, and Ronnie Sadka. 2007. "Seasonality in the Cross-Section of Expected Stock Returns." *AFA 2006 Boston Meetings Paper*, July. Available at: lcb1.uoregon.edu/rcg/seminars/seasonal072604.pdf.

Ritter, Jay. 2003. "Behavioral Finance." *Pacific-Basin Finance Journal* 11(4), September: 429–437.

Sharpe, William. 1994. "The Sharpe Ratio." *Journal of Portfolio Management*, Fall. Available at: www.stanford.edu/~wfsharpe/art/sr/sr.htm.

Singal, Vijay. 2006. *Beyond the Random Walk*. Oxford University Press, USA.

Schiller, Robert. 2007. "Historic Turning Points in Real Estate." Cowles Foundation Discussion Paper No. 1610. Available at: cowles.econ.yale.edu.

Schiller, Robert. 2008. "Economic View; How a Bubble Stayed under the Radar." *New York Times*, March 2. Available at www.nytimes.com/2008/03/02/business/02view.html?ex=1362286800&en=da9e48989b6f937a&ei=5124&partner=permalink&exprod=permalink.

Taleb, Nassim. 2007. *The Black Swan: The Impact of the Highly Improbable*. Random House.

Thaler, Richard. 1994. *The Winner's Curse*. Princeton, NJ: Princeton University Press.

Thorp, Edward. 1997. "The Kelly Criterion in Blackjack, Sports Betting, and the Stock Market." *Handbook of Asset and Liability Management*, Volume I, Zenios and Ziemba (eds.). Elsevier 2006. Available at: www.EdwardOThorp.com.

Toepke, Jerry. 2004. "Fill 'Er Up! Benefit from Seasonal Price Patterns in Energy Futures." *Stocks, Futures and Options Magazine*. March 3(3). Available at: www.sfomag.com/issuedetail.asp?MonthNameID=March& yearID=2004.

Uhlenbeck, George, and Leonard Ornstein. 1930. "On the Theory of Brownian Motion." *Physical Review* 36: 823–841.

Van Norden, Simon, and Huntley Schaller. 1997. "Regime Switching in Stock Market Returns." *Applied Financial Economics* 7: 177–191.

About the Author

E rnest P. Chan is the founder of E. P. Chan & Associates (www.epchan.com), a consulting firm focusing on trading strategy and software development for money managers. He also co-manages EXP Quantitative Investments, LLC and publishes the Quantitative Trading blog (epchan.blogspot.com), which is syndicated to multiple financial news services including www.tradingmarkets.com and Yahoo! Finance. He has been quoted by the *New York Times* and *CIO* magazine on quantitative hedge funds, and has appeared on CNBC's *Closing Bell.*

Ernie is an expert in developing statistical models and advanced computer algorithms to discover patterns and trends from large quantities of data. He was a researcher in computer science at IBM's T. J. Watson Research Center, in data mining at Morgan Stanley, and in statistical arbitrage trading at Credit Suisse. He has also been a senior quantitative strategist and trader at various hedge funds, with sizes ranging from millions to billions of dollars.

Ernie received his undergraduate degree from the University of Toronto, and master of science and doctor of philosophy degrees in theoretical physics from Cornell University. In recognition of his expertise in statistical data mining, he was invited to serve on the Program Committees of the International Conference of Knowledge Discovery and Data Mining in 1998 and also of the SPIE Conference on Data Mining and Knowledge Discovery in 1999. He was also invited to speak at the panel on Effective Arbitrage Strategies at the ETF Evolution conference in New York in 2007.

Index